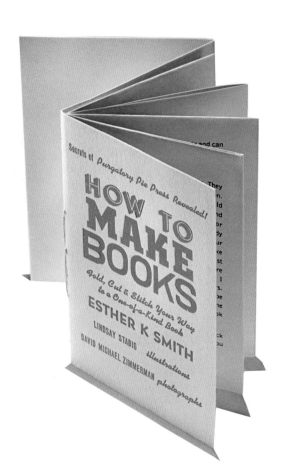

Secrets of *Purgatory Pie Press Revealed!*

HOW TO MAKE BOOKS

Fold, Cut & Stitch Your Way to a One-of-a-Kind Book

ESTHER K SMITH

LINDSAY STADIG *illustrations*

DAVID MICHAEL ZIMMERMAN *photographs*

MAKE book

photographs David Michael Zimmerman

How to

sther

illustrations Lindsay Stadig

KSmith

POTTER CRAFT

LEFT: *Purgatory Pie Press
and Georgia Luna Smith Faust,*
Everything Falls into Place.
*Deluxe do si do binding, handset type,
letterpress, linocut, collage cover.*

Copyright © 2007 by Esther K. Smith

All rights reserved.

Published in the United States by Potter Craft,
an imprint of the Crown Publishing Group, a division of Random House, Inc., New York.
www.crownpublishing.com
www.pottercraft.com

POTTER CRAFT and colophon, and POTTER and colophon are registered trademarks of Random House, Inc.

Library of Congress Cataloging-in-Publication Data is available upon request
ISBN 978-0-307-35336-8

Printed in China

Illustrations by Lindsay Stadig, © 2007 by Lindsay Stadig
Photography by David Michael Zimmerman, © 2007 by David Michael Zimmerman
Book design by Esther K. Smith with handset letterpress typography by Dikko Faust, Purgatory Pie Press,
and graphic design by Kathleen Phelps

10 9 8 7 6 5 4 3 2 1

First Edition

For D!kkO

POLLY
Ella Nora
&
g GEORGIA LUNA

Chapter **4** PAMPHLETS
& chapbooks

Chapter **5** MuTaNT BooKs

Chapter **6** LONG STITCH

Chapter **7** COPTIC

Introduction

Books are containers. They hold things: pictures, words, information. What will your book contain? It could have pockets for business cards and receipts, or ideas and intentions, or fortune-cookie fortunes and exotic candy wrappers. It could hold your poems, your drawings, your secrets.

How to Make Books contains photographs of artist books from Purgatory Pie Press, where letterpress printer Dikko Faust and I collaborate with other artists and writers. Dikko has also handset vintage wood type for the cover and chapter openers. The seven chapters each show a new book structure with projects for you to make. The instructions start with simple, quick projects. First, there are the books that you can make from a single sheet of paper and publish instantly. Then come the more complicated single-signature bindings, what I call the building blocks of book arts: accordion, stab, and pamphlet bindings. Investigate their potential. Once you have made them, try their variations and design your own. You can do so much with these forms. In chapter 5, combine these bindings to make mutant books with wild and creative possibilities. The last two chapters contain longer, multisignature projects using the medieval long-stitch and the ancient African Coptic. Once you become aware of these bindings, you will find them in places like the Byzantine, African, and Asian galleries of the Metropolitan Museum of Art.

Make your books your own, not an imitation of me. What story do you need to tell? What picture do you need to draw? What papers can't you part with? What scraps compel you to create a collage? Make these books fast the first time. Do not start to design until you've made at least one ugly one. Go through the motions. Get the feel of it. When I try a new form with another book artist, we tear up magazines or junk mail, quick fold some signatures, and try a new stitch. The point is to learn how to do it, to get it into our fingers and brains. We save the hard part, the creative part, to do later, back at our studios where no one is watching.

What skills will you need to make these books? You should be able to thread a needle and do some simple sewing. You should know how to cut with scissors, fold with confidence, and tear with verve. If you are good with an X-Acto knife, excellent, but it's not necessary for these bindings. You will need a few simple tools: a bone folder, a cheap awl to punch holes, sharp scissors, linen thread (NOT dental floss), and needles with big enough eyes for your thread. Most projects don't require glue. You can use recycled paper bags, drawing and printmaking art papers, or expensive handmade papers. For a limp-vellum cover, recycle an old leather thrift-store skirt. Instead of jewel-encrusted gilded-leather-covered boards, try linoleum floor tiles or industrial rubber. Steal your methods from every place and every era. Use them as the person you are today.

This may be your first time trying book arts. But maybe you already work with your hands—knitting or cooking or folding origami. Maybe you are a graphic designer who wants to escape from the virtual to make something real. Or maybe you have already tried bookbinding, but you want a fresh approach. Whatever your experience, Welcome! And as they said at the summer camp where I used to work: The first rule is to have fun. (Though, at the pool, my top priority was not to let anyone drown.) Luckily you cannot drown in handmade books. Read your glue labels— one of my students had this odorless clear stuff that looked edible, but the fine print was terrifying. Use good ventilation. Don't cut yourself. Keep fingertip bandages around in case you do.

Fold, cut, score, tear, stitch—explore!

OPPOSITE: *EK Smith, long-stitch box book.*
RIGHT: *Pugatory Pie Press and Susan Happersett,* **Infinity Remove***. Letterpress, die cut, silk-covered boards, accordion binding.*

9

Bill Fick's

G-Squirt

HIGH
ANXIETY

PURGATORY PIE PRESS

Purgatory Pie Press NYC

Hey Suze

Chapter 1

INSTANT BOOKS

MY FIRST INSTANT BOOK came in the mail in 1988. I was a young mother then, living in a fourth-floor walkup apartment in lower Manhattan. I lugged my baby and stroller down the stairs and checked my mail on the way to the park. There was something from Ted Cronin. He had an artist-book gallery that showed our work above a plant store in New

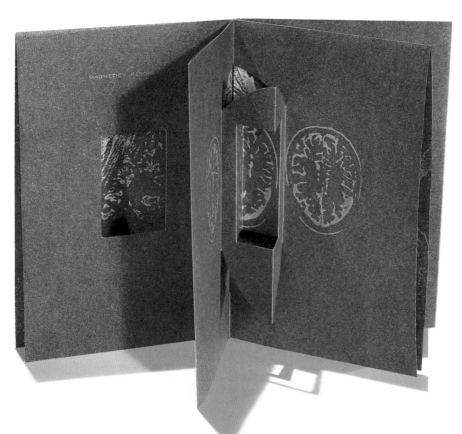

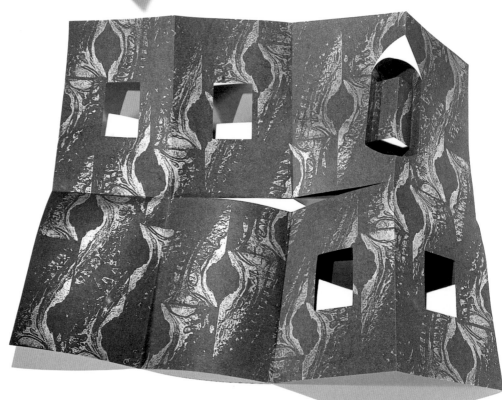

York's flower district—you walked through an urban forest of potted trees and up a back staircase to the gallery. It smelled wonderful there.

I opened my envelope from Ted as I walked along pushing the stroller. I was amazed. It was a little book, made from a folded piece of photocopied paper with a slit in the middle. When we reached the corner, a guy handed me a yellow advertising flier. While we waited for the light to change, I folded the flier, tore the slit, and voilà—an instant book!

Since that first book in my mailbox, I have seen this simple form in many sources and heard it called many things—an origami book, an eight-fold book—but I will always call it an instant book. Its simplicity is its charm. I have made them from sugar-packet papers in restaurants, from the backs of "Hello My Name Is" stickers in meetings, from huge pieces of brown wrapping paper, from pages of promotional calendars, from the fronts and backs of posters that weren't interesting enough to hang on the wall. I even made two from cloth with appliqué images—a baby book and then an abstract version from a worn-out yellow tablecloth.

- -

OVERLEAF: *Purgatory Pie Press and Bill Fick.* **High Anxiety/ Team Evil**. *Handset type, linocut.*
OPPOSITE: *Purgatory Pie Press and Jessie Nebraska Gifford.* **Brains & Spines**. *Handset type and letterpress MRI films with die cuts.*

Basic Instant Book

These are very, very easy, once you get the hang of them. Their three spreads, or six pages, plus front and back cover, will not intimidate even the shyest author or artist. One-sided, they can be published in a minute or two by pressing the button on a photocopier. Yet I find myself going back to them—at Purgatory Pie Press, we have even begun making a limited-edition collaborative series subscription called InstaBooks.

First make one, just to get the feel of it, from anything you have lying around that can be recycled, such as a piece of computer paper printed on one side or a yellow flier that someone hands you on the street.

1 Fold the paper lengthwise, and open. Burnish with a bone folder each time you fold. {A}

2 Fold the paper horizontally. {B}

3 Fold the two open ends up to the middle, front and back. Then open those folds. {C}

4 Tear or slit along center from middle to fold, as shown. {D}

5 Grasping both sides of middle from slit, pull apart and down. {E}

6 Fold into a book form. {F}

You will notice that your book's pages don't line up perfectly. The reason is paper thickness. The thickness of a piece of regular 8$\frac{1}{2}$ x 11" (21.5 x 28cm) printer paper seems almost nonexistent. But think about how thick a ream of that printer paper is, or a novel—or a phone book or a dictionary. Paper thickness adds up, even in this very simple book.

You cannot trim this book, because it will fall apart, though you can round the corners. If you want it to be even on the edges (often I don't care if it is), you need to make an allowance for the paper thickness. Do this on the second fold, the first horizontal fold. Do not fold it exactly in half; instead leave about $\frac{1}{4}$" (6mm). If you are using thicker paper, allow a little more space. I always experiment with the paper first, before I start a real piece of art.

Before you begin, understand that this simple book is what it is. You will learn to make other books in later chapters that may be more satisfying, but none will be more instant. Enjoy this instantness, and see what you can do with it. If you publish an instant zine, send me a copy to add to all the ones my students have made over the years.

YOU WILL NEED

One 8$\frac{1}{2}$ x 11" (21.5 x 28cm) sheet of lightweight paper

Scissors

Bone folder

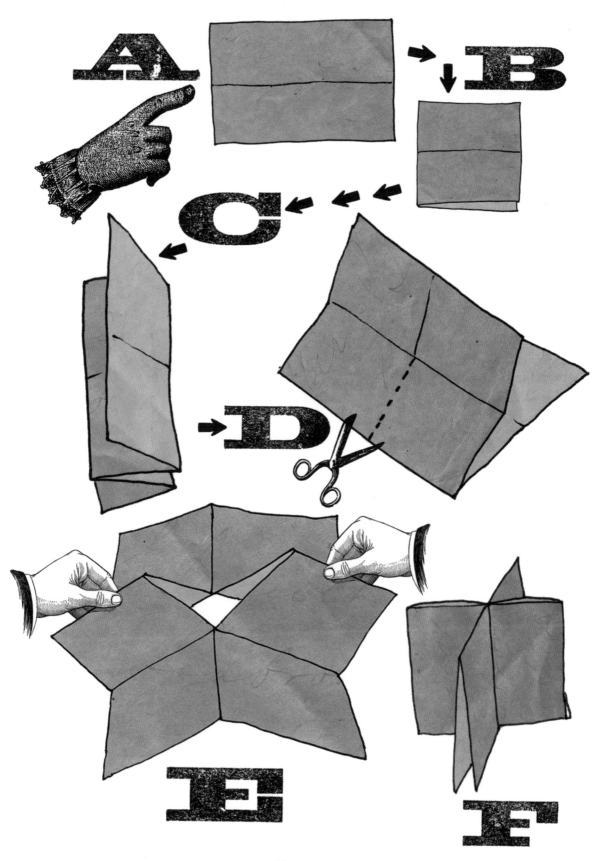

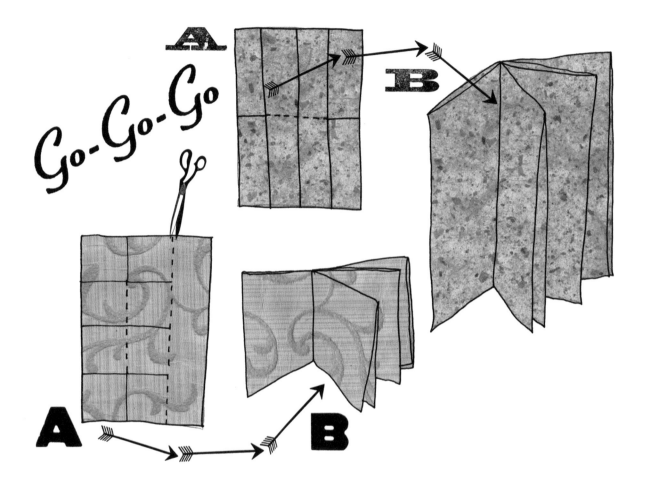

TALL AND SQUARE INSTANT BOOKS

Instant books can be excellent for amusing children. It's fun to see what they will draw on their books. If they are too young to fold and cut, they can still illustrate them. If they are too young to write, they can tell you their stories and you can write captions. If they are too young to draw, they can delight themselves scribbling. Folding instant books from paper wtih random scribbles and other abstract drawings already on them can be very interesting—you can either leave the pages as is or continue to "work into them" as they say in pretentious drawing circles. Instant books make excellent mail art. Imagine opening your mailbox and finding an instant book in addition to your bills and junk mail and credit card offers! Just follow the illustrations above to make the tall (top) and square (bottom) versions of the Basic Instant Book (page 14).

Instant Zines

Zines are little self-published magazines, usually made at work, while on the clock, using the company photocopier and whatever paper is available for free. I do not recommend stealing from your employer—I only mention this as a convention of underground publishing! I've been told zines started in the 1950s in sci-fi circles.

YOU WILL NEED

Desired number of 8½ x 11" (21.5 x 28cm) sheets of lightweight paper

Scissors or X-Acto knife

Bone folder, fingernail clippers, or paperclip

Photocopier

Some zines are fanzines. Others are political, about radical vegetarianism, the World Bank, or conspiracy theories. Still others are art. Make 'em, collect 'em, trade 'em.

BELOW: Susan Happersett. *Fibonacci Is Watching You*. Color-photocopied instant-book zine.

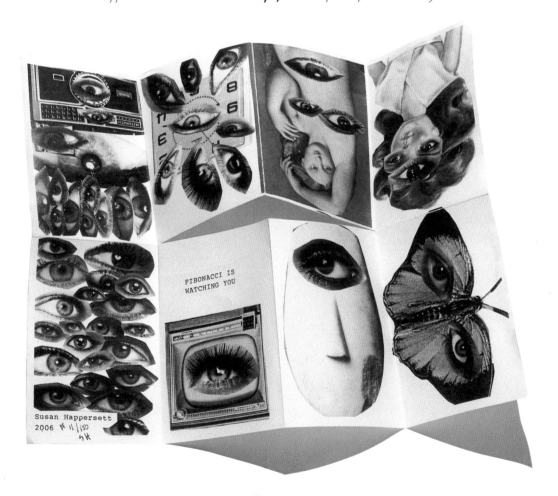

There are many ways to publish on a photocopier—I recommend that you experiment (I always recommend that you experiment). If you need to use a commercial copy shop, try to find one with nice people who will try things for you.

1   Empty your pockets. Try using fortune-cookie fortunes for text, or cut words from magazines, newspapers, or damaged books. Illustrate with charms, charm bracelets, or antique brooches. Try photocopying flowers, crumpled and then flattened paper, leaves, dead bugs, glass objects—see what you get. I read about a sign from a country barbecue joint that said, "If it fit on the pit we will barbecue it." It became one of my many mantras.

2   Lay the contents gently on the glass of the photocopier. Press PRINT and see what emerges. Fold the paper as for the Basic Instant Book (page 14). What random pages appear? Or cut up the bits that you like and tape them into an already-made book to create a story.

3   What looks interesting from your experiments? Plan and design your zine from there. When you are ready, lay things directly on the machine and try copying it. Adjust for darkness. Experiment with papers, colors, and whatever textures will go through the photocopier.

The term *camera ready* is becoming obsolete, but if you are using a black-and-white copier, it's an important concept to understand. Your original must be black on white, even if you want to later print it on bright-colored paper. If you are having children make these books and you want to be able to copy them, give the kids soft black pencils, black ballpoint pens, grease pencils, or markers to work with. I don't recommend Sharpies because I hate the toxic smell, but a water-based marker with a similar line quality works well.

You can, of course, use a color copier or a computer printer in the same basic way. Always test your paper for both printing and folding before you begin a project of multiples. "Measure twice, cut once," as carpenters say.

When editioning zines, experiment, test, and make dummies early in the process to avoid having to solve problems when it's too late to start over. (A dummy is a sort of sketch or working model of a book that you use for planning and design.) Some commercial paper companies provide designers with paper for testing.

BONE FOLDERS

The bone folder is the most basic binding tool. Use it for scoring, folding, tearing, burnishing, rubbing, and embossing. When you first get a bone folder, wash it in soapy water and scrub well. Then dry it and soak it in cooking oil overnight to make it more supple. Wipe it off and let it dry so that it absorbs the oil. The first time you use your bone folder, try it on cheap paper to be sure it is dry. Keep some fine emery paper on hand to sand your bone folder if it chips. Always burnish your folds with a bone folder, protecting your book with a clean piece of scrap paper. If you have a silicone folder, you do not need the waste sheet because silicone will not mark the paper. But silicone folders cost about five times as much.

In a typical Purgatory moment, I was scoring a pop-up for a book (it was an expensive Japanese paper that we bought to fake newsprint—funny how you fake cheap things with expensive things in archival book production). The paper folded so easily that I was quite impressed with my scoring. Of course it was too good to be true. My bone folder had a little chip—I realized it when I ran my finger over it and felt the rough place. Instead of scoring, it had cut almost through the paper. My friend KK came to the rescue with document repair tape. We were able to reinforce those scores, which saved the edition.

THIS PAGE: *Kathleen Phelps, scanner zines.*
Inkjet printing.

ONE-OF-A-KIND INSTANT BOOKS

If you are not trying to publish your books on a black-and-white photocopier, you have more freedom to try many other papers.

A large piece of brown craft paper can be interesting to play with to make a huge book. You may need an assistant—think how hard it is to fold a beach blanket by yourself.

Follow steps 1–6 for the Basic Instant Book (page 14).

If the paper is difficult to fold, score it with a bone folder and a straightedge. Try rectangular shapes in different proportions and see what you get. How low can you go? Can you make a book so small that you need a magnifying glass to read it (and to write it)? There is a big market for miniature books.

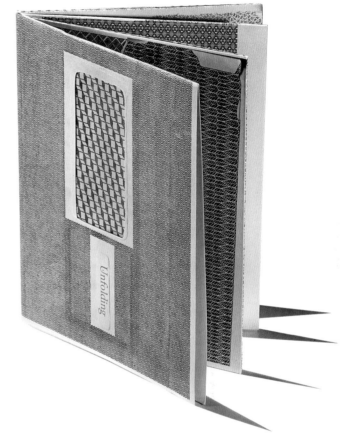

ABOVE: *Elizabeth Duffy, sketch/dummy for Purgatory Pie Press InstaBook series. Data-protection patterning on envelope interiors.*

Illustrate with collage, rubber-stamping, drawing, and/or painting. You can insert photos using photo-safe double-stick tape, an archival glue stick, or photo corners. Make sure to burnish well with a bone folder, protecting the page with a clean waste sheet.

Experiment and have fun.

One artist showed me a variation in which she intentionally did not line up the paper exactly when she made the first fold. The result was modern sculptural skewed form. She used it for her Christmas cards.

Cloth Instant Book FOR BABIES OF ALL AGES

My first cloth instant book was a baby-shower present for one of my interns. I used reproduction African animal print—blue figures on an off-white background. I cut them up and placed them on muslin, making a very simple visual narrative. I imagined the soon-to-be-born baby pointing to the lions and porcupines.

Combining disparate elements in a surreal composition, such as a tiny mammal with a huge flower, is a good technique for cloth books. Try making a collage from the images on cloth. You can look in fabric stores, buy bales of old kimonos, ask your sewing and quilting friends for scraps, cut up old clothes, or sift through yard sales or thrift stores to find fodder for your art. Like a quilt, this project could be a delicate wedding coverlet or a utilitarian object. Think about your audience when you choose your fabrics.

One morning, as I was going through some summer clothes, I found an old square-dance dress that I hadn't worn for years. I had loved it in college—it was a hand-me-down from my friend Margie. I vaguely remembered that it had torn. And indeed the bodice was in tatters (though I probably could have made a circle skirt from the bottom). But suddenly I was glad—I'd been looking for highly illustrated fabric to make a cloth book, and the little dancers on the dress were perfect. Not only did I get something that I needed, but my tattered vintage dress may live on in an artist book.

1 Begin this project as for the Basic Instant Book (page 14). Fold the background material lengthwise, spray with water, iron, and open.

2 Fold crosswise, spray, and iron.

3 Fold both ends toward the middle, spray, iron, and open.

4 Cut a slit at the center from the middle fold to the first fold. {A}

YOU WILL NEED

Large rectangular piece of background material (16 x 24" [40 x 61cm] makes a 6 x 8" [15 x 20cm] book)

Assorted patterned fabrics for cloth collage

Scissors

Pins and safety pins

Iron and ironing surface

Spray bottle with clean water

Needles and threads

Sewing machine (to work quickly; optional)

Iron-on adhesive or fusible interfacing (optional)

Rubber stamps, fabric markers, or fabric paints (optional)

Buttons and beads (optional)

Stuffing or quilt batting (optional)

5   Grasp the fabric on both sides of slit, pull open, and fold into a book shape. {B}

6   Spray and press along each fold. {C, D, E}

7   Now the fun begins! Cut out figures and designs from your fabrics. Leave room for a seam allowance around the image ($^1/_4$" [6mm] is enough) in case you decide to really go for the craft and hem your pieces.

8   Pin the designs onto your book. This is your chance to try things out. See what looks interesting by moving the pieces around.

Alternatively, you could skip the fabric entirely (and the next few steps) and make your book content with rubber stamps, paints, or drawings. If the book really isn't meant for young children, you could even make a paper collage.

9   After you pin your collage, unfold and flatten your book and then decide how to adhere and finish the book. {F} Think about how much time you are willing to commit and how the book will be used. If it is a piece of art that will be handled gently, you can leave interesting raw edges. If a young baby will play with it and chew on it, the book needs to be washable, and you should take a more heavy-duty approach.

The quickest, easiest way to attach your collage is to iron it on with fusible interfacing.

With a little more time, you can stitch the pieces on with a sewing machine. If you use a very close zigzag stitch, you don't even need to turn under your raw edges (which is what I did for my last-minute baby book). If you'd rather have a more finished look, pin the raw edges under, press them, and then machine-sew with topstitching or zigzagging.

If you really want to invest a lot of time and make this an heirloom sort of project, you could hand-stitch your appliqués and embellish them with embroidery. {G}

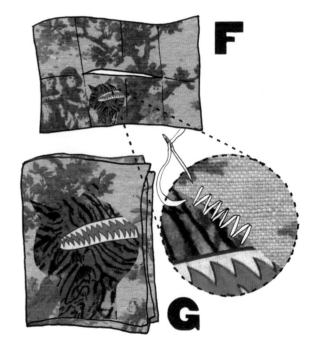

10 Finish your design with buttons and beads, unless it is likely that this book will be chewed and buttons possibly swallowed. You can also embroider a text or other embellishments.

11 When your have attached your collage, fold the cloth back into a book form and press again.

At this point, if you want the book to be a little puffy or less floppy, you can add interfacing (fusible or not) or a little stuffing or quilt batting between the book's pages.

12 Sew the edges shut, either zigzagging or turning in the raw edges and topstitching.

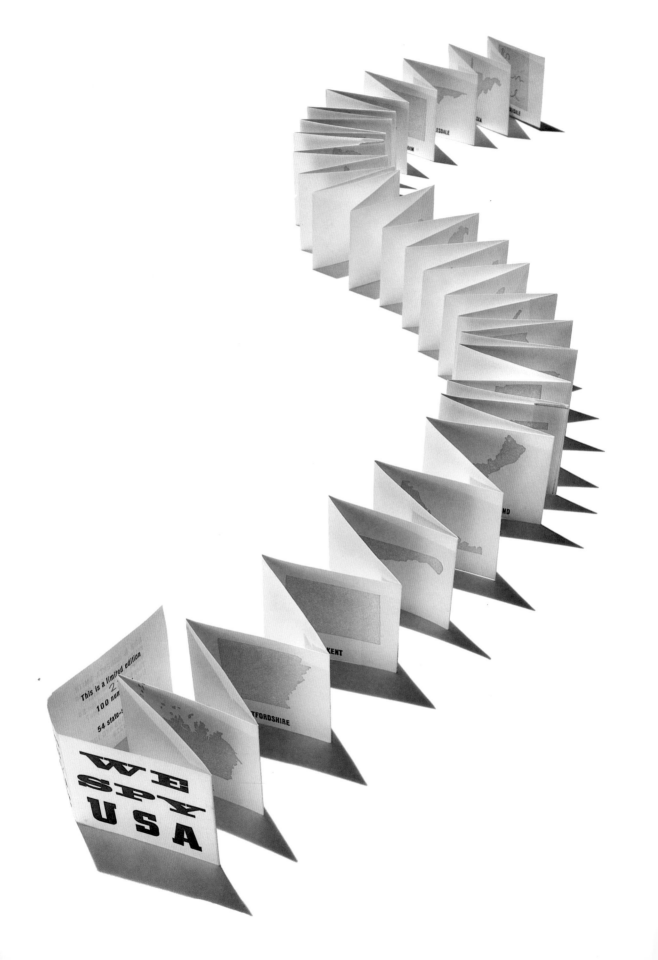

Chapter 2

ACCORDIONS

ACCORDION BOOKS LOOK EASY. There is no real mystery; they make intuitive sense. But they are trickier to make than to understand. It's not a forgiving form. It demands precision—small discrepancies in folding multiply as you go.

I began to appreciate the accordion structure in the context of exhibits. A Purgatory Pie Press book called *Lily Lou* was exhibited at the Center for Books Arts in New York, and Dikko and I found an angry note in the guestbook from a man who was very upset that he couldn't read the whole story. My first response was, *Why don't you just buy the book—support an artist for a change.* But it got me thinking about the challenge of exhibiting books. Books are intimate objects—you need to hold them, manipulate them, turn the pages. There are solutions to this problem. At a MoMA exhibit, I virtually turned pages of a few Russian books with interactive computer screens. In some exhibits, videos or automated slides show you the pages. Other times, white gloves are provided, and you can touch the books with supervision. If you are exhibiting books that already exist, these options may be the only way to show their pages. But if you are making books you intend to exhibit, it is worth thinking about how they will be shown in a gallery. Even if you are making a book to commemorate a family reunion, you may still want to be able to display it. One way to show all the pages in a case (or on a shelf or wall) is to use the accordion format.

- -

OVERLEAF: *Purgatory Pie Press and Bob & Roberta Smith,* **We Spy USA**. *Handset metal type, letterpress, linocut.*
OPPOSITE: *Purgatory Pie Press and Michael Bartalos,* **Laocoon & the Double Helix**. *Handset metal type, neoprene plates.*

Three Instant Accordions

When Purgatory Pie Press had an exhibit at Harvard, we went up to teach a weekend letterpress workshop at the Bow and Arrow Press in a Harvard building at the corner of Bow and Arrow streets. (I think of it as our Winston Churchill Memorial/Blood, Sweat, and Tears Letterpress Boot Camp Workshop.) Bow and Arrow Press had a collection of nineteenth-century wood type and several printing presses, but it lacked some necessities. There was no paper guillotine, and for edition books, you need be able to cut whole stacks of paper. One of the students rescued the workshop with this very cool accordion-book form. You fold your paper into quarters both vertically and horizontally, and then cut, alternating from side to side. It saved the project. We made a book about leap year that weekend.

Like the instant book, this form isn't perfect. But it's easy to do with just a bone folder and sharp scissors.

To learn the basic form, use office paper or any lightweight paper. Remember to burnish your folds as you go, always protecting your book with a clean piece of scrap paper.

YOU WILL NEED

One 8½ x 11" (21.5 x 28cm) sheet of paper

Scissors or X-Acto knife

Bone folder

1 Fold the paper in half crosswise and then fold both sides up to the middle {A}, open it, and flatten. *Note:* Flattening the paper before proceeding is important, because the folds should only be the thickness of one sheet of paper for accordion books.

2 Then fold vertically in half and fold both ends to the middle {B}. You will have sixteen pages.

FOR THE FIRST VERSION

3 Cut in a spiral starting at the first fold in the upper right corner. {C}

4 Fold, reversing folds as necessary until the book is complete. {D, E, F, G}

FOR THE SECOND VERSION

3 Cut from the left side, stopping at the first right fold. {H} Then cut from the right side, stopping at the first left fold, and then from the left side again, as shown. {I}

4 Fold, starting at the top corner, reversing folds as you go. {J}

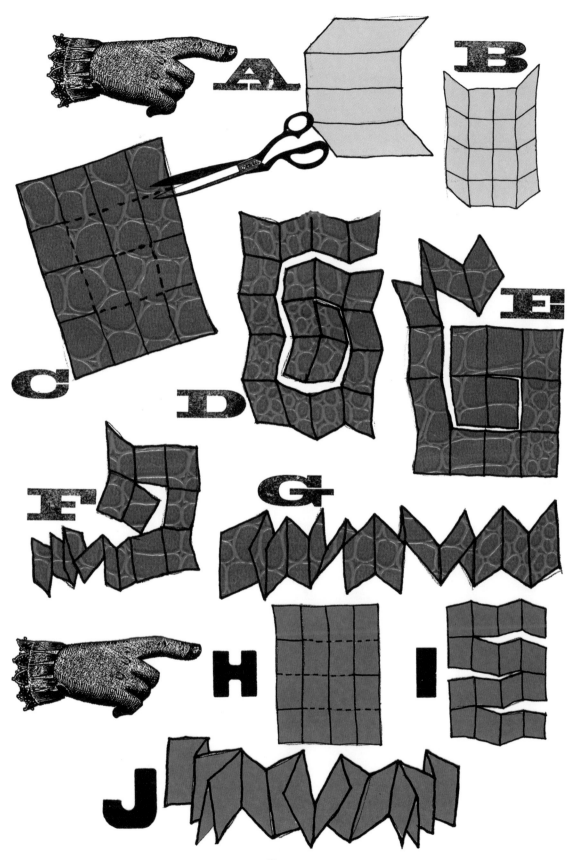

A

B

C

D

E

F

G

H

I

J

3 Follow the instructions for folding and cutting in version two {A, B} but cut vertically instead of horizontally. {K, L}

4 Fold, following the instructions for the second version. {M}

5 Follow the instructions for weighting your book (below). {N}

These instant accordions are a little clumsy at the corners—sometimes I dab some glue there—but they are quick and easy and fun.

Once you understand these instant structures, try them with nicer paper. Since the paper needs to fold with and against the grain, use something that folds both ways—a light cover stock or heavy text-weight paper. Like the Instant Book (page 14), any size square or rectangle can work.

You can easily publish these 8½ x 11" (21.5 x 28cm) versions with a photocopier.

Make some light pencil markings on your dummy to see how the pages will work when they're unfolded (some will be upside down). Then switch to clean paper and make your camera-ready version (if you are using a black-and-white photocopier) with collage or drawings. Photocopy one, then adjust as needed. Photocopiers aren't completely accurate, and your results will vary from day to day, so don't plan something that will make you miserable if it shifts a little here and there.

Book Weights

After folding an accordion, you may notice that it doesn't want to stay folded. You need to press accordions under weight to instill molecular memory.

You can buy a book press at an antique store or flea market—it looks like a wine press, only smaller. Or weight your book with a cold flat iron—those antique irons that were once heated on an old iron stove. One student of mine makes book weights by filling Altoid tins with pennies. Some binders wrap bricks or cinderblocks with cloth or heavy paper, gift-wrap style, and adhere with tape or glue. In *The Perfect Spy* by John le Carre, the protagonist's wife is a bookbinder. She uses her husband's old socks to cover bricks for her book weights—a quick method!

At Purgatory Pie Press, when we are making editions, we fold all the books, spread them evenly on a counter, put waste sheets on top, and then lay metal galleys of heavy type on top to press all the books at once. We have a small binding press, but it won't hold enough books at one time to be useful for a limited edition.

For a single book, you can cut two pieces of heavy cardboard the size of your book and tie it tightly around or secure it with multiple rubber bands. I've used this method when I've shipped books before they were weighted sufficiently (after having the recipient swear to keep the book under weight when it arrived).

Keep the book under weight until it no longer expands when released. A few hours, overnight, several days, a week—the longer the better.

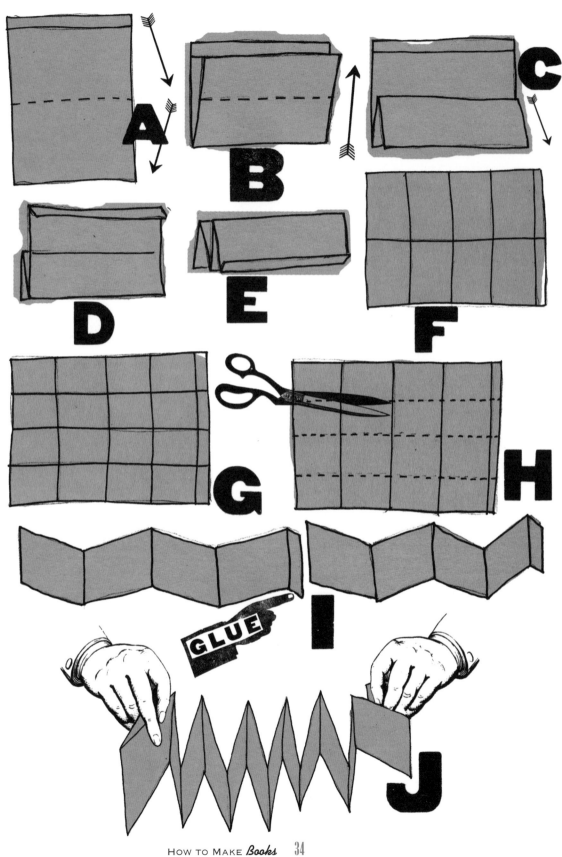

Self-Hinged Accordion Dummy

This quick exercise shows you one way to make an accordion that is longer than your original piece of paper. Although there are quite a few kinds of papers that you can buy in rolls, you may want to work with sheets of flat paper. Just to get the idea, make a quick dummy of this one with your handy letter or scrap paper.

1 Fold a little hinge—about ½" (13mm) across the short edge of your paper. {A}

2 Fold the bottom end up to the fold. {B}

3 Fold that end back to the middle, as shown. {C}

4 Do the same on the back, folding from the middle to the hinge fold. (D, E)

5 On the vertical, fold as you did for the Instant Accordion (page 14): in half and then both ends into the middle. {F, G}

6 Cut into vertical strips, as shown, leaving a hinge on the end of each strip. {H}

7 Glue or tape together at hinges {I} to make one long accordion. {J} There will be one extra hinge, which you can chop off or use to glue the book to a cover.

Another approach is to take a few strips of paper and start folding a page size that pleases you or with dimensions that are right for the content you plan to include—with a margin around photos or postcards, for example. When you have accordion-folded the whole strip, it may come out even, but you will probably have a piece left over. You can use that as a hinge if you need to attach other folded strips to make your book long enough.

HINGE OPTIONS

If your page paper is too thick for self-hinging, make hinges (think of these like strips of tape) from lighter, strong pieces of paper—Japanese papers are great for this. Prefold these hinges, trim to the page height, and line them up with the edges of the two pages you want to join. Adhere with paste, glue, or archival double-stick tape.

I have experimented with having hinges show, using them as interesting visual elements in the book, like newel posts on a stairway (I often think of books in architectural terms). Try making tall hinges with interesting shapes—just be sure that the hinge lines up at the bottom so that the book can stand.

YOU WILL NEED

1 piece of 8½ x 11" (21.5 x 28cm) office paper or other scrap paper

Bone folder, fingernail clippers, or paperclip

Scissors or X-Acto knife, straightedge, and cutting mat

Glue stick or archival double-stick tape

SPINES

Spines make it possible for you to find books on a bookshelf. As I write this I am working on the design of this book's spine—I am hoping to make it an open spine with exposed stitching and a small label with the title and necessary info. (Take another look at it now and see if my publisher agreed with me!)

At a Small Press Center Book Fair, I met a publisher whose books were straightforward, but there was something I really liked about their design. She said she had worked in advertising, but left Madison Avenue to start a small regional Hudson River Valley history imprint. She told me that the spine was the most important part of the book. In bookstores, most books are shelved spine out. This publisher said her modest publishing venture never expected to have their front covers shown—that bookstore space is taken up by bestsellers and celebrity tell-alls. She said she would pay much more for cover images—a tall ship mast or a mountain peak—that would look intriguing when wrapped around the spine.

ABOVE: *Purgatory Pie Press,* **Candace's K–1 Class Picture Alphabet.** *Letterpress from Styrofoam drypoint and handset wood and metal type.*

Since then, I've been more aware of spines in bookstores and in the library. The spine entices you. It makes you pull the book off the shelf.

In your own home library, a book without a spine gets lost. *The Washington Cornmeal Company Cookbook* is my favorite baking book. It has some easy cakes, an impressive four-minute fat-free fluffy frosting, and good muffins and biscuits. But it's a stapled pamphlet, so I can never find it. If you can't find a book, does it cease to exist? It's like that silent tree that falls in the woods when no one is there to hear it. Well, now we are getting into philosophy—but seriously, folks!

COVER WITH SPINE

1 Starting at the front edge, lightly wrap a strip of cover-weight, short-grain paper around the spine of your Self-Hinged Accordion Dummy (page 34). (The paper should be short grain so that it folds without cracking.) {A}

2 Open the cover-weight paper and score the width of your spine using a metal triangle. Then fold the cover to fit. {B}

3 Glue the extra accordion hinge on your book left from the margin, into the fore edge {C}, spine {D}, or back edge {E} of the cover, trimming excess as necessary.

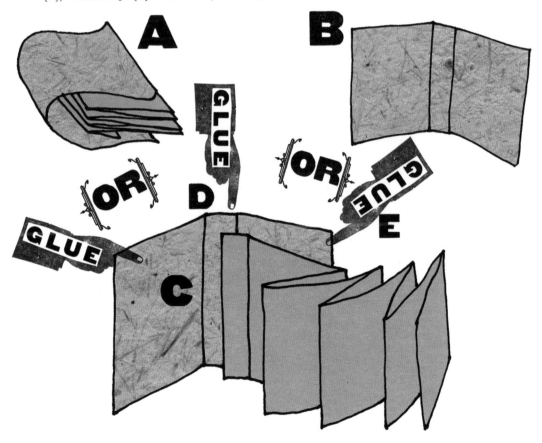

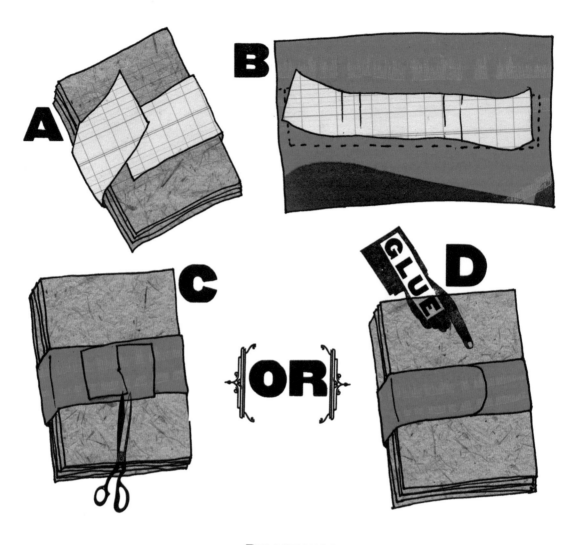

BELLYBANDS

Accordion books are springy, so you need to weight them until they relax (page 33). This may take a few days. After the bounciness is weighted down, you can make a bellyband, cover, or slipcase to hold the book together. If you do this before the book is weighted, the bellyband or cover will be too big once the paper accepts its new shape.

1   Lightly wrap the book with a strip of scrap paper to make a pattern, allowing extra length to secure the band. {A}

2   Trace around the pattern with a bone folder or pencil. {B}

3   Score using a metal triangle for straight folds.

4   Slit {C} or glue {D} the top and bottom halfway so that they slide together, as shown.

POCKET COVERS

If you'd like your accordion to be bound into a cover, you can glue one in at one or both ends (page 37). Or you can have your cake and eat it, too, by making a removable cover with flaps that fold in and pockets for the ends of the accordion to slide into. Slip the cover on to read your book by turning pages, or slide it out one side or both and stretch to display on a shelf, mantel, or glass case.

1   Take a piece of cover-weight, short-grain paper, about 4 times the width of the interior pages and 2" (5cm) taller. Score the cover and fold around the spine, front and back, creating flaps like those on a dust jacket.

2   Trim the front, back, and spine to the same height as the accordion. The flaps will be ³/₄" (2cm) longer on the top and bottom.

3   Fold in the top and bottom of the flaps and glue them to make pockets for the accordion ends.

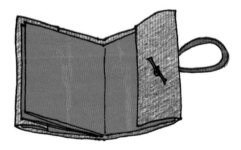

COVER WITH ELASTIC

1   Fold a cover with a spine and flaps, as above.

2   Using an awl, punch a hole for the elastic and insert, as shown, from the inside back cover to attach accordion into cover.

ABOVE: *Lindsay Stadig, sample Accordion Postcard Album using antique French postcards.*

Accordion Postcard Album

I have collected postcards for years. My collection started when I was in a tiny junk store with some college friends in Wisconsin and I found a 1920s hand-colored postcard of my very dull hometown a thousand miles away. There were also postcards of the shredded wheat factory in Niagra Falls and other odd subjects. They were within my budget, which meant dirt cheap at the time (and isn't much better now!), so I bought them, sent the one of the factory to my parents—not sure that they appreciated its humor—and started my collection. That was when I first got the concept of kitsch. Postcards soon piled up, and I didn't know what to do with them. If I had had *How to Make Books* then, I would have made this handy accordion postcard album.

This album holds standard 4 x 6" (10 x 15cm) vertical postcards or photographs, but you can alter the slits to work on another size. Because it is glueless, the album will not damage the cards or photos, which you can interchange with care.

Before you begin making the book, practice cutting and folding the windows.

1 Cut a gig, or pattern, from a piece of heavy board that is a bit smaller than your postcard. Think of this as the opening of a mat or frame. So, for a 4 x 6" (10 x 15cm) card, your gig should be $3^1/_2$ x $5^1/_2$" (9 x 14cm). This is your cutting gig. {A}

2 Cut a larger second gig from the heavy board. This will be the outer dimension of your postcard. This is your folding gig. {B}

3 Before cutting into your accordion, practice this mat-cut on a piece of heavy cover paper that is light enough to fold when scored.

4 Place your smaller gig in the center of the paper. Trace the gig firmly with your bone folder. {C}

5 Take an awl and pierce each corner. {D}

6 With a metal straightedge and an X-Acto knife (sharp fresh blade, please!) and using a rubber cutting mat to protect your table (and also to grip your paper), cut an X from

YOU WILL NEED

Piece of heavy board

A sheet of heavy but foldable short-grain paper

Strong, lightweight paper, if accordion paper is too heavy to self-hinge

X-Acto knife, metal straightedge, rubber cutting mat

Bone folder

Needle or awl

Glue, paste, or archival double-stick tape

Heavy cover paper, for practicing mat-cut and for cover

Cloth or paper for outside of cover

Ribbon or ties

Paper always folds better in one direction than the other. It tears straighter in that same direction, too. This is because the fibers line up during paper manufacture, creating grain.

When you are figuring out your paper grain, don't trust your eyes. The paper may be wider on one side, and it may seem like such a good idea to fold it in half that way, but if the grain is long, instead of a squarish rectangle you may end up with something inconveniently tall and thin. When I was helping bind books in a subbasement of the Metropolitan Museum or Art, another binder showed me her method for determining paper grain. She would close her eyes or look away and sort of bounce the paper in both directions, relying on her sense of feel to tell the difference. Another approach is to cut off a few small pieces, or swatches, marking them to indicate which way they fit on the large sheet. But here are a few other methods:

METHOD 1. Dampen the paper and see how it curls. It will curl on the grain as it dries.

METHOD 2. Try tearing the paper in both directions—ever notice how hard it can be to neatly tear a story out of a newspaper or magazine? One way will tear pretty straight—with the grain. Against the grain, the tear will be hard to control.

Always check paper grain before you start your book, and design with that in mind.

The paper needs to fold on the grain, which will eventually be parallel with the book's spine.

diagonal corner to corner, both ways. {D}

7 Fold back these triangle tabs and burnish with a bone folder. {E}

8 Place the larger folding gig over the window, with tabs evenly showing around edges. {F}

9 Fold back tabs over the gig. {G}

10 Gently remove the gig and place the postcard or photo in its place. {H}

MAKING THE ALBUM

11 Using the illustrations on page 34 as a guide, cut wide strips of heavy but foldable short-grain paper. These should be taller than the height of your postcards. Fold $1/2$" (13mm) on one end to self-hinge. If your paper is too heavy to self-hinge, you can make hinges from a strong, lightweight paper.

12 Fold the strips into an accordion. Make as many of these as you need to for your postcards. Because the book will be thick, do not plan to put more than fifteen or so postcards inside.

13 Join your folded accordions together with their hinges. You can use paste, glue, or double-stick tape. Be sure to burnish well. Let your paste or glue dry under weight.

14 Fold your whole accordion together and weight.

15 Decide where your postcards will go. If they will all be in the same location on their respective pages, you can use an awl or needle to mark the corners through the whole book, or several layers, depending on its thickness. Cut your mats, fold, and insert the postcards.

16 Cut a piece of board to the size of your page. Adhere to the front and back of the accordion, sandwiching ribbons or ties between the cover and the book if you want to tie it shut. Weight the book.

MAKING A SLIPCASE

17 Measure around your finished book: front, spine width, and back, with spine width above and below.

18 Score and cut out a cover from heavy stock, leaving a curve to pull out the book at the fore edge. {I}

19 Adhere the top and bottom layers. {J}

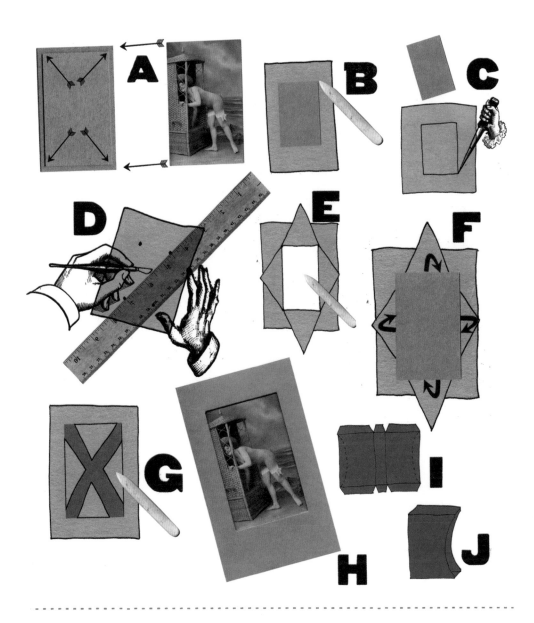

- -

WORKING WITH PAPER

"I cut my cote according to my cloth" is a quote that I found when I was a costume designer, researching ancient clothing. In different parts of the world, people used different loom widths, and so their clothing styles were based on that wide or narrow cloth. Some clothes would be strips pieced together; others would be wide, draped, flowing clothes.

Now, please mentally leap from cloth to paper (and from sleeves to hinges). Yes, you can go out and buy a specific paper for a specific project—and when I'm making an edition, that is what I do. For some projects, when the budget's good enough, I work with papermakers designing custom paper, but even then, they have standard screen sizes. But when I'm designing, I start with what's lying around. I "cut my cote according to my cloth," and make my book according to my paper.

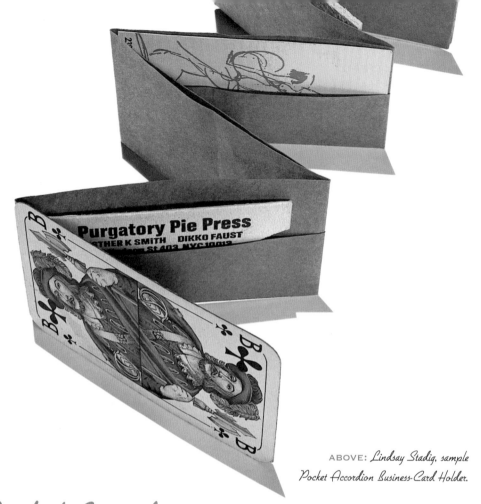

Pocket Accordion BUSINESS-CARD HOLDER

Since accordions can fold both ways, they make interesting pockets. You can use these pocket accordions many ways—for store receipts and other bits of paper or for creative projects, where interesting things (like instant books) emerge from the pockets. Think of them as traveling art and information systems. Toss this business-card holder in your bag or briefcase or slip it into your front pocket.

YOU WILL NEED

A wide strip of paper that is thin enough to fold in both directions, 1½ times the height of a business card

Bone folder

Cover pieces cut from cover-weight paper or board

Double-sided tape or glue stick

Ribbons, ties, or elastic

1 Cut the paper to approximately 3¼ x 30" (8.3 x 76cm). Measure 1" (2.5cm) from the bottom, and fold the entire width of the paper to make the pocket flap.

2 Accordion-fold this piece a little wider than a standard business card, leaving a short fold at both ends to secure the ends. {B, C}

3 Affix cover pieces with tape or glue. *Note:* You can add ribbons, ties, or elastic between covers and accordion. {D}

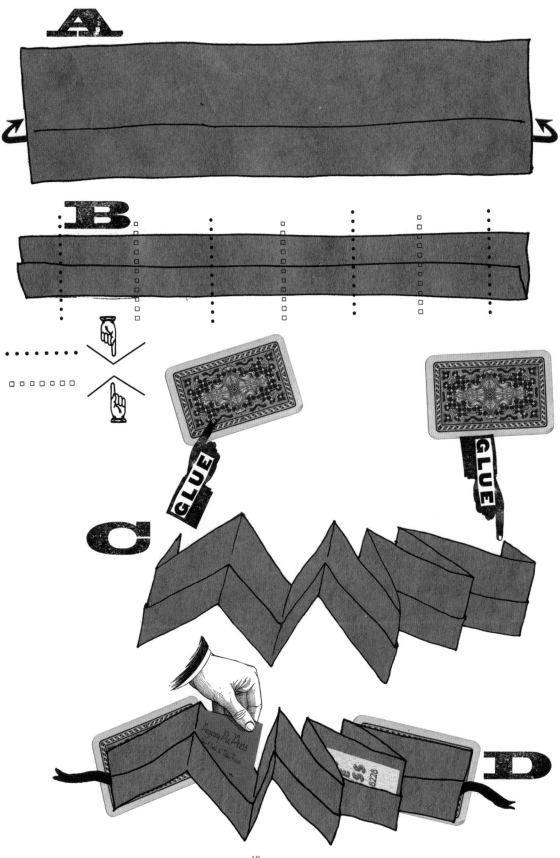

Chapter 3

STAB ▸ STITCH

STAB STITCHING IS OFTEN CALLED Japanese binding, though it is just one of many Japanese bindings, and it really started in China and is also used in Korea. There are variations in the different countries (there is even a Dutch version, as you will see), but they are all basically the same.

At first, I did not like stab-stitch binding, and then, as so often happens, I learned from a student. Betty Harmon disregarded my instructions for the simple three-hole binding and instead stitched enchanting thread drawings. Later, I saw some artists working with this form using thin, strong, limp Japanese papers. They worked beautifully. And it made so much sense—Japanese binding from Japanese paper! Cloth books have that same drape and flow that can open flat even with a stab-stitched spine, in case you'd like to make another Cloth Instant Book for Babies of All Ages (page 22).

At Purgatory Pie Press, we use stab stitching for binding jobs. We bound one hundred poetry books as wedding favors. We used stab stitching to bind an artist's flipbook edition. We taught forty-nine sixth-graders to stab-stitch their own yearbooks (see photo, opposite).

Setup for stab stitching is time consuming. Don't let that frustrate you. Or if it does, don't let your frustration discourage you. Allow plenty of gutter margin at the spine, and make sure that your paper grain goes with your spine. Punch your holes with an awl. If your book is too thick for the awl, divide it in sections, and use a sheet from the first section as a guide to punch the other sections.

If you are binding a whole edition, you should drill your sewing holes, clamping your book well so that the drill doesn't grab it and send all the pages flying. (How would I know about this? There is a reason we named our press Purgatory!) Protect your book from bruising and marking from the clamps with waste sheets and pieces of cardboard.

- -

OVERLEAF: *Purgatory Pie Press, one-of-a-kind notebook. Wood type, stab-stitched binding.*
OPPOSITE: *Purgatory Pie Press and Hunter College Elementary School sixth-graders, yearbook. Handset type, letterpress printing, stab-stitched binding.*

Recycled-Paper Book

We all end up with so much paper. Maybe it's the invention of the photocopier. I am a college professor, and every time I check my mailbox it is brimming with one-sided notices, most of which are irrelevant to me. A few months ago, a grant proposal was due, and I had a problem with Microsoft Word. It made every paragraph into a separate page, so my five-page document printed out as fifty pages. Yes, this paper could go into the recycle bin or a landfill—after all, it's only trees—but I prefer to use it. Making books from scraps can be a good way to give a tree a second chance. When you make this basic stab-stitched dummy, remember: The paper grain must be parallel with the spine.

1   Fold the 8$\frac{1}{2}$ x 11" (21.5 x 28cm) paper lengthwise, and burnish with a bone folder.

2   Using scissors or an X-Acto knife, slit the paper on the fold. {A}

3   Fold the sheets in half so that each one is 4$\frac{1}{4}$ x 5$\frac{1}{2}$" (10.75 x 14cm), printed side inside. {B}

4   Cut and fold the cover sheet the same way. You will have two folded covers, one for the front and one for the back.

5   Stack the folded sheets with the covers on the front and back, the eight text sheets in the middle, and open ends on the left, folds on the right. {C}

6   Using the bulldog or binder clips, clip this pile on the top and bottom, protecting the cover with extra paper to prevent bruises from the clips.

7   Score a line on the left side of the cover $\frac{1}{2}$" (13mm) from the edge with your bone folder.

8   Punch three holes using the awl on the score: one in the middle, one $\frac{1}{2}$" (13mm) from the top, and one $\frac{1}{2}$" (13mm) from the bottom. {D}

YOU WILL NEED

4 or more sheets of 8$\frac{1}{2}$ x 11" (21.5 x 28cm) lightweight office paper, printed on one side

1 sheet 8$\frac{1}{2}$ x 11" (21.5 x 28cm) colored cover-weight paper, preferably already printed on one side

X-Acto knife

Bulldog or binder clips

Awl

Needle

Waxed linen thread

Bone folder

9   Start sewing in the middle hole. {E} Hold the tail of your thread, and sew through and around the spine, leaving 3" (7.5cm) at the end for the final knot.

10 Bring the thread back up through the middle hole, then sew down to the bottom hole, sewing through the spine and around the bottom. {F–J}

11 Sew back to the middle and up to the top, sewing around the top. {K–P}

12 Sew back to the middle to tie off your thread with a square knot. {Q} Your thread should never be doubled, and all spaces should be filled. {R}

13 Release the book from the binder clips or bulldog, open it, and press down, rubbing, so that the pages "know" how to open.

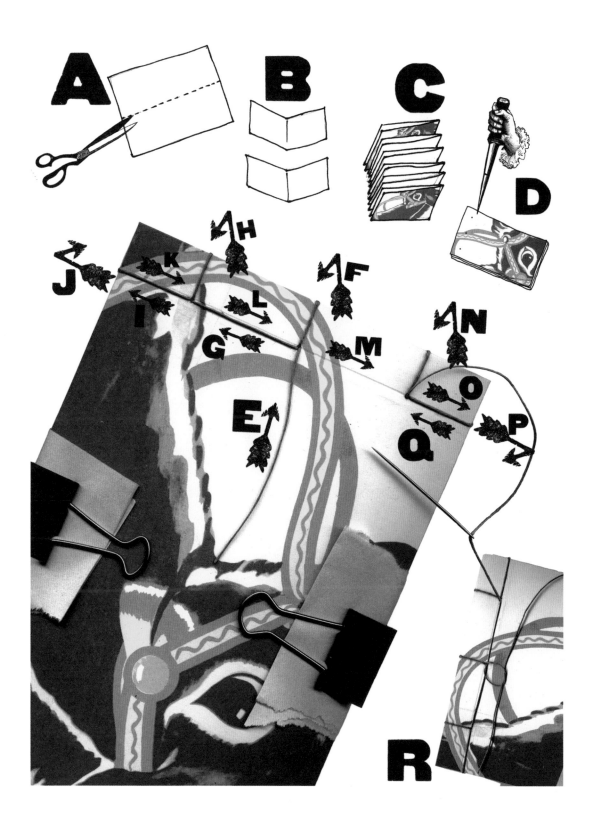

Slack Stab-Stitched Recycled Book

A few years ago, a Dutch artist showed me Dutch binding. It looked like Japanese binding to me, but there were small variations—the stitching, for example, did not wrap over the head and tail of the book. The 1920s Dutch artist magazine *Wendingen* was bound this way with a charming stitch variation. The thread crisscrosses three pairs of holes, going around the spine in a three-dimensional cross-stitch.

Browsing at the Strand bookstore in New York City, I found a book with an interesting spine. I pulled it out, and it turned out to be a book about contemporary Dutch artists, sewn with a loose stab stitch. The pages were printed on one side of wide sheets and folded. The folds of the sheets were at the fore edge. The open ends of the sheet were loosely stab-stitched at the spine, like a stitched accordion. I thought its slackness was a mistake. But I bought it. It was cheap. And I was interested to see the binding used in that context. Later I saw that the loose stitch was not a mistake—it allowed the book to open flat.

For this version, you can use slick thread or satiny ribbon, if it passes the thread strength test (page 54), to encourage the pages to slide over the thread. Try this binding with shoelaces and leather cords—or whatever seems strong enough and looks interesting with your project. Make your sewing holes large enough to allow for thread motion and to accommodate the thicker ribbon or cord.

1 Fold the 8¹/₂ x 11" (21.5 x 28cm) paper lengthwise, and burnish with bone folder.

2 Using an X-Acto knife, slit the paper on the fold.

3 Fold the sheets in half so that each one is 4¹/₄ x 5¹/₂" (10.75 x 14cm), printed side inside.

4 Cut and fold the cover sheet the same way.

5 Stack the folded sheets with the covers on the front and back, the eight text sheets in the middle, and the open ends on the left, folds on the right.

6 Using the bulldog or binder clips, clip this pile on the top and bottom, protecting the

YOU WILL NEED

4 or more sheets of 8¹/₂ x 11" (21.5 x 28cm) lightweight office paper, printed on one side

1 sheet of 8¹/₂ x 11" (21.5 x 28cm) colored cover-weight paper, also printed on one side, if possible

Bone folder

X-Acto knife

Awl

Bulldog or binder clips

Needle

Thread, ribbon, shoelace, or leather thong

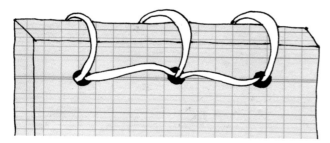

cover with extra paper to prevent bruises from the clips.

7   Score a line on the left side of cover $1/2$" (13mm) from edge with bone folder.

8   Using the awl punch three holes on the score: one in the middle, one $1/2$" (13mm) from the top, and one $1/2$" (13mm) from the bottom. Make sure the holes are big enough to accommodate your thread—they should be larger than the holes you made for the Recycled-Paper Book (page 50).

9   Start sewing in the middle hole. Hold the tail of your thread and sew through and around the spine, leaving 3" (7.5cm) at the end for the final knot. As you sew, keep your tension loose by gently turning the pages and opening the book flat (almost like a loose-leaf binder) to be sure you have enough slack in the stitching for the book to open this way.

10   Bring the thread back up through the middle hole, then sew down to the bottom hole, sew around the spine, but not around the bottom.

11   Sew back to the middle and up to the top, sewing through and around the spine, but not over the top.

12   Sew back to the middle. Your thread should never double. All the spaces should be filled.

13   Open and close the book gently, working the slackness of the thread to be sure you have enough so that the pages can open flat.

14   Tie a square knot. Tuck in your thread ends, if you like.

- -

ABOUT THREAD

Use linen bookbinding thread. Some art and craft stores sell it on cards, but if you find that you like to sew books, for a little more money, you get much more thread when you buy spools of it. You can get spools at bookbinding specialty stores, like Talas in New York City. I mail order from a basketry supply store in Ohio called Royalwood—they give you a discount when you spend $50.

You can buy waxed thread, wax your own, or work with unwaxed if you prefer. Waxed thread is stronger, which is good when your thread is exposed on the spine, and it does not tangle as easily. I love waxing my own. I get my beeswax from honey sellers at the farmers' market. A lump of wax will last a few years. Beware of dental floss and other suspect suggestions on the Web. Some people believe that dental floss is a good alternative to waxed linen. It is not.

Before you use thread to bind a book, you should test it. I bound an entire edition of one hundred datebooks with a spool of orange linen thread I'd had since my costume-design days. It broke. I resewed the books that came in for repair, but of course some people didn't tell me—and others were treasuring their datebooks instead of using them.

To test thread, wrap it around the fingers of both hands. Pull as hard as you can without cutting your fingers. If it breaks, don't use it. You don't absolutely have to use bookbinding thread, but use something that will not break.

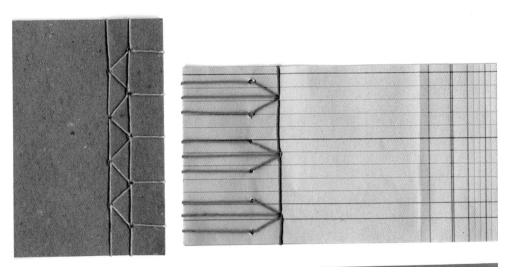

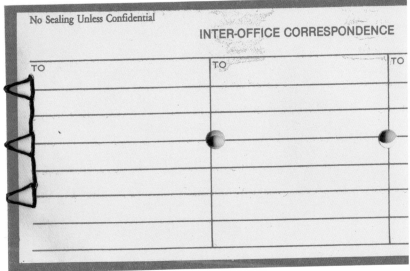

STAB-STITCH PATTERNS

There are many traditional stab-stitching patterns (some examples shown above) and many contemporary versions, like spiral and loose-leaf binding. Something as simple as a staple on the top corner of a four-page syllabus is a form of this stitch. Once you understand basic binding, try some of the stitches shown in the illustrations above. Then try making up your own. You can, of course, vary your paper size and texture. Limp, soft Japanese papers that flow instead of resist opening are the ideal paper choice for stab stitching.

Envelope Book

I like envelopes. I look for them in old office supply stores when I go to out-of-the-way neighborhoods. I found some nice ones in a not-for-tourists newsstand in Chinatown a few months ago. Whenever I get interoffice envelopes, I do not cross out my name and keep them going. Instead I collect them and sort of treasure all those different offhand written notations in all those different pens—and the paper buttons and the strange punched holes.

I incorporate envelopes into bindings when I need them. They are useful in datebooks or for storing receipts, odd business cards, or stamps. Use them to hold postcards, and keep them with you in case you have a few minutes while waiting somewhere to write a note to a friend, a kid in college, or someone else who might enjoy something real in their mail for a change.

This project is made up of envelopes, the kind that close with a button and string and reopen easily so that you can store your collage materials, organized by category for future artist books.

1 Pile your envelopes with flaps on the right side facing up, and clip them together with binder or bulldog clips.

2 Score or fold a line on the top envelope about 1" (2.5cm) from the left side (which will become the spine).

3 Using the awl, punch holes along the left side, 1" (2.5cm) from the top and bottom and several evenly spaced between—the number will be based on your pattern. Punch at least five holes.

YOU WILL NEED

5 or more string-and-button closure envelopes (approximately 9 x 12" [23 x 30.5cm]), like interoffice envelopes

X-Acto knife (optional)

Bulldog or binder clips

Awl

Needle

Heavy, waxed linen thread

4 Stitch according to your chosen pattern.

5 Make labels for whatever you plan on organizing. You can either write them or collage the envelopes for visual clues.

ABOVE: *Lindsay Stadig, sample Envelope Book.*

THIS PAGE: *Dikko Faust and EK Smith, sample Group Book. Drawings by Georgia Luna Smith Faust, pastepaper-covered board, linen thread.*

Group Book: GIFT FOR A TEACHER

Teachers' gifts can be difficult. An aunt of mine taught for thirty years and had the knickknacks to prove it. As a child, I was delighted because at every visit to her in Philadelphia, I could choose something from the shelf in her china closet. But as an adult, I feel her frustration as more and more junk piles up in the finite space of a city apartment. I remember her saying, "Don't give me anything I cannot eat up or use up." That's probably a good rule of thumb for teachers, but sometimes you want to give something very meaningful. Still, the problem remains: What do you give to the person who has too much of everything? A book, of course! You can organize it so that each child makes a page or several pages on a theme, then bind them together for a unique work of art and love. Looking at it years later will bring vivid memories of the children who participated with their words and pictures.

BOOK PAGES

1 Remove sheets from pad.

2 Line up the side of metal ruler along the top edge and score each sheet ruler-width, then fold that edge back. This is the no-man's land of the book—it must be kept blank for the spine sewing.

3 Distribute pages to the participants, explaining the no-man's land and telling them to work horizontally on one side only of the sheet, with the hinge on the left. You may want to distribute a diagram to clarify the instructions. You could choose a theme, such as dinosaurs, an apple-picking trip, or favorite memories from that school year.

The artists can work in a variety of media—watercolor, colored pencil, markers, and pens. If they are using collage, you will need additional strips the same size as the folded hinges to make more room at the spine. You want the thickness at the spine to at least equal the thickness of the pages.

When working with groups, especially children, make the pages in the classroom instead of sending them home. Have extras

YOU WILL NEED

1 pad of 9 x 12" (23 x 30.5cm), lightweight, multipurpose paper

Metal ruler

Bone folder

2 pieces of decorative 11 x 14" (28 x 35.5cm) paper for covers

Two 9 x 12" (23 x 30.5cm) boards—one can be from the back of the paper pad

2 pieces of contrasting paper for the cover end sheets, or decorative paper

2 pieces of 11 x 14" (28 x 35.5cm) colored or decorative paper

Adhesive (PVA or sheets or double-sided tape)

X-Acto knife

Drill

Bulldog or binder clips

Waste paper

Needle and thread

of everything, and decide up front whether or not the artists can print their texts on the computer.

Overeager adults can spoil children's work by trying to make it look "professional." One of my favorite artist collaborators, Stephanie Brody Lederman, talks about "the mark of the hand," which is what is so wonderful about children's art. Sometimes adults try to make something look childlike by strewing pictures at angles. This is meant to look casual, but it just looks bad. How things are placed on the page—the composition of the negative space as well as the positive—is an important, intuitive decision. Children and other artists need a good atmosphere and structure for their work—plus encouragement and support—but don't do it for them; trust them.

BACK FLAT COVER

1   Lay decorative paper (at least 1" [2.5cm] larger than the boards on all sides) color side down.

2   Adhere the back board to decorative paper, centering with 1" (2.5cm) of the decorative paper around all sides. {A}

3   Fold the edges of decorative paper around the board, burnishing with the bone folder. Remember to protect the paper with a waste sheet.

4   Unfold and trim (miter) the corners of the decorative paper, leaving a little more than the thickness of the board at the corner (use the fold marks to guide you).

5   Adhere the top and bottom edges, folding over the corners and burnishing with the bone folder.

6   Adhere the sides the same way.

HINGED FRONT COVER

1   From the edge of one sketchbook back board, cut a strip the same width as the page hinges (approximately 2" [5cm]).

2   Cut a piece of decorative paper that is about 2" (5cm) longer and 5" (12.5cm) wider than the front cover.

3   Adhere the large piece of front cover to the back side of decorative paper with the X-Acto knife, leaving a 1" (2.5cm) margin on the right side, top, and bottom, and 3–4" (about 8cm) on the left for the hinge. {C}

4   Adhere the 2" (5cm) hinge strip on the left side, leaving about ¼" (6mm) between it and the large cover piece for easy motion. This space must accommodate the thickness of the board plus the decorative paper.

5   Fold decorative paper edges over the board and trim (miter) the corners as you did for back cover.

6   Adhere the top and bottom edges as for the back cover, working the decorative paper into the space between the hinge and book with a bone folder.

7   Adhere the sides as for the back cover.

ENDSHEETS

After you've made both covers, you'll want to line them with single end sheets. {B, D} These can be more decorative papers trimmed a bit smaller on all sides than the covers. Then weight the covers overnight or for a few days. Protect them with clean paper, cover with heavy boards, and place weights on top, peering in at eye level to make sure the weights are on top of the covers at important places, like at the corners and hinge.

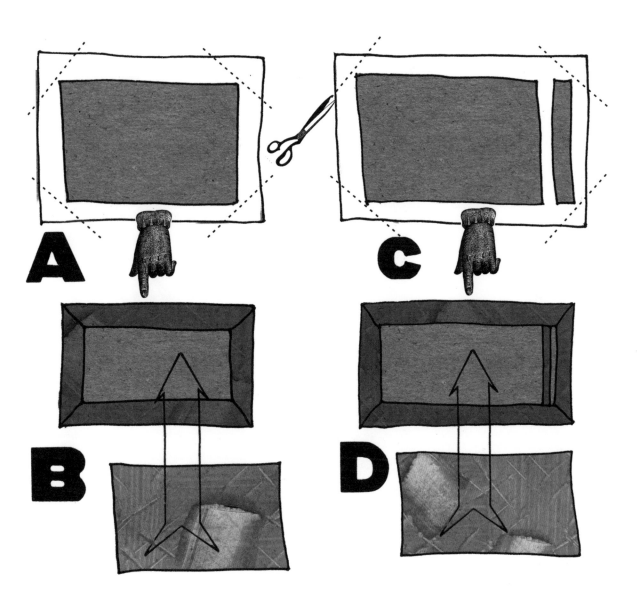

A

B

C

D

STITCHING

1 Pile the pages, making sure that all folded hinges are flattened and on the same side and that the pages are in the right order. {E}

It makes sense to have a title page at the beginning, and you could even make a table of contents, a colophon, and list of contributors.

You can have someone do these pages by hand, especially if you're working on a one-of-a-kind book. Beware of bad calligraphy, though—the kind you get when someone's aunt has a wide-nib pen. Even professional calligraphy can look pretentious and wrong for this kind of project. But unaffected, readable handwriting can be very nice. Older people sometimes have beautiful penmanship, since it was taught in school before personal computers.

When we worked with a group on a project like this, we designed the title page, handset the type, and letterpress printed it, which is always a great option in the unlikely event that you have letterpress access. You may have a good graphic designer in your midst who can help with typography.

2   Place covers on the top and bottom of the pages, and make sure that the front is on the front and the back is on the back. (This may seem silly, but remember, measure twice, cut once. We once had an intern who bound twelve books upside down!) {F}

3   Clamp the book on the bottom with a board that can be drilled into and a piece of wood or Plexiglas on top. Mark your holes (you can predrill through your top piece) and drill through the book. {G}

4   Stab-sew as you did for the earlier books in this section. Choose or design a stitch pattern that looks interesting in the context of your project.

You can make variants of this book to commemorate significant birthdays, anniversaries, and other major events and as thank-you gifts. It's also a way to make a yearbook (photograph on page 48).

One of our clients ordered a *New York Times* front page from every significant date in his father's life to commemorate a big birthday ending in zero. Our calligrapher wrote out the dates and their corresponding events (his graduation, wedding, births of children, and so forth) on translucent sheets of paper. We laid those over the corresponding newspaper pages and then stab stitched them into a large, weighty, leather-covered tome.

PUBLISHED VARIATION

It can be nice to edition a group book, so that each contributor can have one. Since the pages will have to be photocopied, plan it for 8½ x 11" (21.5 x 28cm) paper, or a smaller size that can be trimmed from standard printer or copier paper.

Have the participating artists draw and write with black pens and markers, or soft black pencils (4–8B drawing pencils) if they are willing to draw dark lines. They should leave a 3" (7.5cm) margin on the left for binding and 1" (2.5cm) on the other three sides, since photocopiers have problems printing close to the edges. Though the originals must be black and white to be camera ready, you can print onto any color or texture paper that will feed through the machine. Experiment with a few options before you print the whole book.

If you have the budget for color photocopies, you can use color on the originals. A few color pages among black and white can be effective and elegant. I always ask new groups of students if anyone has free use of a color copier—you might know someone, too.

One way to make a group book look consistent is to design it so that pictures go in the same position on every page, giving it a visual rhythm.

The covers for this version can be simply made from cover-weight paper. Touches like decorative end sheets can give each book a unique element.

- -

HOW TO LOCK THREAD ON A NEEDLE

To lock thread onto a needle, backstitch through a tail on the thread, as shown. If your thread is very heavy and very waxed, just folding it back, pinching, and pressing it with your fingernail may be enough to keep it threaded. Do not sew a book with the thread doubled.

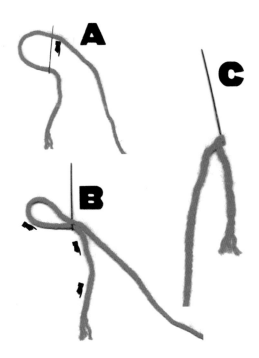

Stab-Stitched Cloth Book

Since stab-stitched bindings do not open flat, and the ideal material for them is very limp, they make great cloth books. Like the Cloth Book for Babies of All Ages (page 22), make this as a toy, an art piece, or both.

1 Cut the plain cloth into 8 x 20" (20 x 51cm) pieces. {A}

2 Fold the pieces in half to make 8 x 10" (20 x 25.5cm) pages; spray and press. {B}

3 Pile the pages up with the raw edges on the left {C}, pinning them together on the left side with safety pins. {D} This is your book blank.

4 Make separate covers with the heavier, contrasting cloth, cutting pieces that are slightly larger than your book pages.

5 If you like, use a decorative patterned or translucent cloth (or even lace!) for end sheets. Cut the end sheets to match the size of the interior pages.

6 As for the Cloth Instant Book (page 22), find fabrics with interesting figures, cut them out, and collage them onto the book, pinning as you make creative decisions. Be sure to pin through only one layer of the folded pages at a time.

Note: If you want your pages to have a finished look, you will need to leave ¼" (6mm) around all of the edges for the seam allowance (step 10).

7 You can also draw directly on the pages with fabric markers, paint with fabric paints, or use rubber stamps. Sandwich blotting paper between the folded pages so the ink or paint won't bleed through.

8 When you've arranged all your content, pin on pieces of paper and number the pages so they don't get mixed up (the numbers could remain part of your book, which could be very nice).

9 Remove the safety pins from the spine, flatten the pages, and adhere the cloth collage images. As for the Cloth Instant Book, you can use iron-on adhesive, stitch on the sewing machine, or hand-stitch.

YOU WILL NEED

1 yard of 45"- (114cm-) wide plain cloth, such as heavy muslin, for text pages

1 yard of 45"- (114cm-) wide contrasting, heavier cloth for the covers

1 yard of 45"-(114cm-) wide patterned or translucent cloth for end sheets (optional)

Scissors

Iron

Spray bottle with clean water

Figured cloth for appliqué

Fabric paints, markers, and/or rubber stamps (optional)

Pins and safety pins

Blotting or waste paper

Sewing machine

Needle and threads

Iron-on adhesive

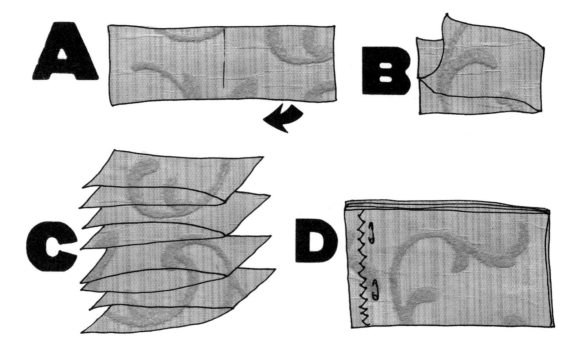

10 After your collage is assembled, sew the pages shut. You can either machine-zigzag around the rough edges or put right sides together, sew the top and bottom, and turn out and press. If you want to take the pillow book idea literally, you can insert stuffing inside the pages before you sew them all the way shut.

11 Decide how you want to finish your pages on the spine. You can fold the raw edges in and press them before you stitch the spine for a finished look, or leave them raw if it suits your content.

12 Pile the pages with your cover and end sheets. Make sure to double-check that they are in the correct order!

13 Sew with one of the stab-stitching patterns or work out your own design. You can also stitch near the spine with a sewing machine, if the book isn't too thick, or sew buttons through the spine, if you like.

- **VARIATIONS** -

NEEDLE BOOK

To make a book to hold needles, just make the Stab-Stitched Cloth Book with smaller pages. You can use any kind of fabric, even felt. Appliqué a collage or design the pages with paints, or just insert your pins and needles in interesting patterns.

ABOVE: *Sarah Ballard, sample Stab-Stitched Cloth Book (interior).*

LUXURY
LIQUID
Shampoo

CONTAINING
Olive Oil and Glycerine

Buerger Bros. Supply Co.
Denver and El Paso

BUERGER'S
Lila

TO
U

ILET
ATER
LILAC FRAGRANCE

MANUFACTURED BY
THE BUERGER BROS.
SUPPLY CO.
DENVER, COLO.

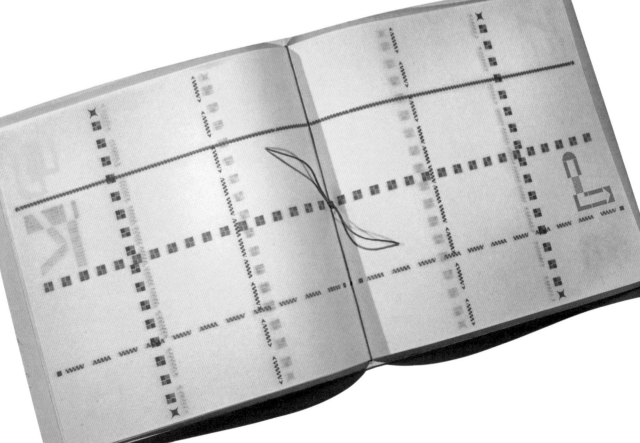

Chapter 4

PAMPHLETS
& chapbooks

SMALL PRESSES OFTEN PUBLISH chapbooks—

cheap booklets of poetry or short stories. I had never known why

they were called chapbooks until someone asked me when we

saw a shelf of them at Spoonbill and Sugartown, a bookstore in

Williamsburg, Brooklyn. I asked the bookseller, who also didn't

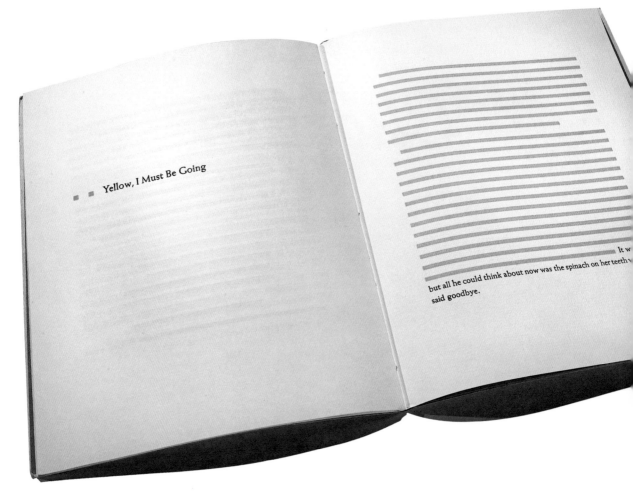

■ ■ Yellow, I Must Be Going

It w

but all he could think about now was the spinach on her teeth said goodbye.

know. He Googled chapbooks—now really, I could have done that!—and it turns out they are called chapbooks because they used to be sold by chapmen. Another Google search revealed that chapmen were wandering peddlers in sixteenth-century England. During the information revolution of the Renaissance, in the early days of post-Gutenberg movable type, books were suddenly accessible to the people, and literacy exploded. Printed broadsides cost half a penny. Chapbooks—the pulp fiction and zines of their day—were available cheaply wherever packets of pins, buttons, and other sundries were sold. Now the words *chapter* and *chap* make sense!

To understand how to make chapbooks and booklets, you first need to know a thing or two about signatures. Fold a piece of paper in half and you get four pages. A signature is a folded section, a few sheets of paper folded in half together and stitched on the spine. A pamphlet book is simply one sewn signature.

Students always ask me how many pages to put in a signature, and I always answer, "That depends." It depends on your paper. Is your paper thick or very thick, thin or very thin? Do you want your finished book to close square, so that the spine is the same thickness as the open edge? Are you planning to collage or place photos on your pages? Four to eight folded sheets is a typical signature for lightweight paper. The thicker your paper, the less pages your signature should hold. In hand-sewn binding, even a single folded sheet of thick paper can be a signature.

It's good to start with a simple pamphlet book. It is a great way to learn to organize pages. Get comfortable folding and organizing. Then learn to make the multisignature books in chapters 6 and 7, where you'll be sewing many sections together.

- -

OVERLEAF: *Purgatory Pie Press*, **Alphabetize**. *Collage cover and letterpress spread with handset metal type and ornaments.*
OPPOSITE: *Purgatory Pie Press and Peter Cherches*, **Colorful Tales**. *Handset metal type and rule.*

Basic Three-Hole Pamphlet

Quick—sew this pamphlet to understand the concept of a single signature. Once you do it, you'll be able to make your own chapbooks. My first book was like this—I made it in kindergarten. It was called "How a Seed Grows" and sewn with red yarn. The teacher wrote all the words and drew the pictures on the blackboard for us to copy—schools did not encourage creativity back then. I didn't learn another book for almost twenty years, but that one was enough. I even used it for my college creative writing projects.

End sheets are my favorite part of a book. In some bindings, they are structural, glued to covers to secure the book. They hide the mechanism of the binding, which some people think is ugly—sometimes it is. But end sheets are also the vestibule. The cover is the door that beckons you in from the outer world into the world inside the book. Interesting endpapers function as the passageway between the worlds—once inside the book, you immerse yourself in its content. Endpapers can be plain text sheets that match the interior of the book. But they can be as flamboyant as you like. Even the dullest, plainest, conventional books can let loose with their end sheets. Like a tie with a business suit, an end sheet can be a vivid touch of color. If your book is very wild inside and out, you might want your end sheets to be the calm element between inner and outer worlds.

1   Fold text paper, end sheets, and cover paper in half on the grain. {A}

2   Punch three holes near the fold with the awl: one in the middle, one about 1/2" (13mm) from the top, and the last 1/2" (13mm) from the bottom. Punch into an open phone book or thick magazine to protect your table.

3   Thread your needle, and start sewing from inside the middle hole, leaving a 4" (12cm) tail of thread. {B} Hold the tail down with your nonsewing hand. Sew back at the top hole, skip the middle, and go out the bottom hole. {C–D} Come back in front again at the middle hole, taking care not to split the thread that's already there. {E}

4   Tie the two thread ends around the long middle piece with a square knot (left over right, right over left). {F} Because the knot is sewn around the other thread, it will not pull through the paper. Paper fibers can separate and open to allow even large knots to work their way out.

YOU WILL NEED

4–8 pieces of lightweight text paper

2 pieces of decorative paper for end sheets, same size as text sheets

1 piece of cover paper, slightly larger than text sheets

Bone folder

Awl

Needle and waxed linen thread

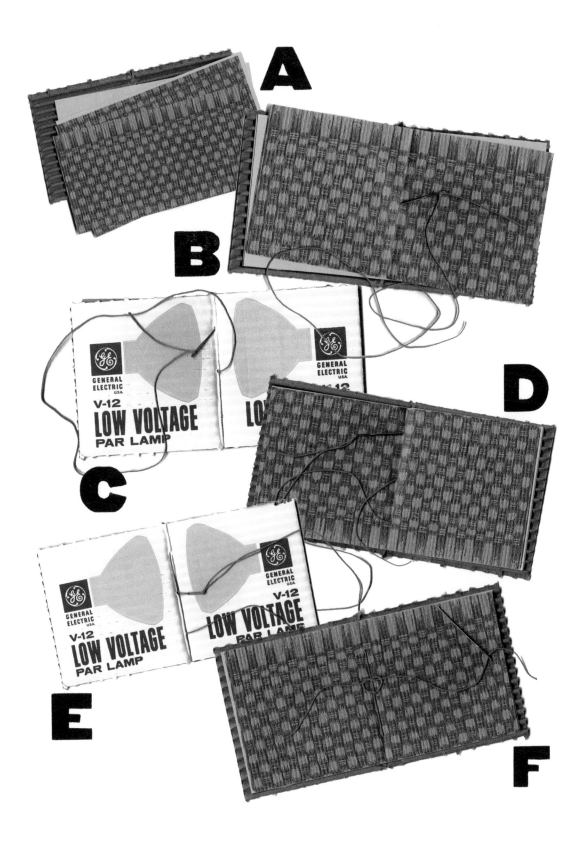

THIS PAGE AND OPPOSITE: *Susan Happersett.*
The ABCs of Beauty*. Collaged photocopy.*

Printed Alphabet Book

Designers make what's called a dummy when planning a book to figure out efficient use of paper and press. Make this alphabet book project to learn this planning process. Alphabet books usually have twenty-six pages or spreads, one for each letter. Books like these are made to help children learn letters and sounds. Others are address books or organizers. Many people collect them.

We made a picture alphabet with Candace Coran's kindergarten/first-grade class when they studied books (photograph on page 36). We wrote the alphabet on the board and let the children choose the letters they wanted. They drew pictures with ballpoint pens onto precut pieces of Styrofoam meat trays that the grocery store's butcher had provided. One child drew "yell" for Y; another drew "quiet" for Q. Evan drew "eating eggs" for E. We printed those "Styro-graphs" on the letterpress. You could print yours by inking the styrograph, laying paper over it, and rubbing it gently.

If you are photocoping, work with a standard size paper: 8½ x 14" (21.5 x 35.5cm) or 11 x 17" (28 x 43cm). Start with that size paper and fold it down to make a page proportion that you like.

12 or so pieces of 8^1/$_2$ x 11" (21.5 x 28cm) white paper
for dummy and original

Desired number of 8^1/$_2$ x 11" (21.5 x 28cm) sheets of
copying paper

Decorative paper for end sheets

Cover-weight paper

Black-and-white collage materials, old magazines, etc.

Paste, glue stick, or archival double-stick tape

Bone folder

Needle

Linen thread

1   Cut or tear four pages of white paper in half cross-wise, to make eight 8^1/$_2$ x 5^1/$_2$" (21.5 x 14cm) pages. {A, B}

2   Fold these pages together into a single signature, temporarily securing it with a rubber band. You will now have 32 pages: Use 26 for the alphabet pages, one for a title page, and the outer pages for the cover (you can either have this book "self-cover" or you can use the two outer pages for end sheets). {C}

3   Lightly number the pages.

4   Pencil in the design for the cover, title page, and letters of the alphabet. {D, E, F}

5   If you like, you can very lightly and quickly sketch your basic plan on the pages.

6   Separate the pages and tape them back into their original 8^1/$_2$ x 11" (21.5 x 28cm) sheets. These will be your dummy, so you will know how to design your actual book before the pages are cut in half. {G–H}

7   With clean white paper, design your book using the dummy book you just created in steps 1–6 as your guide. If the book will be photocopied in black and white, make it camera ready, collaging with black-and-white pictures, drawing with pen and ink or black markers, grease pencils, and/or soft drawing pencils. If you aren't sure how something will photocopy, try it on a machine before you go too far. You can work both sides of your pages or use different pieces of paper for the fronts and backs, as long as you are careful to follow your dummy. Lightly code your pages to indicate which back goes with which front. We sometimes do this with roman numerals and letters, using "I-f" and "I-b" for front and back of the same printed sheet. Make a practice version quickly, so that you are sure you understand how to use your guide and make your pages back up correctly.

8   Photocopy your originals front and back. Remember even though your original must be camera ready, you can use any paper that feeds through the copy machine to make your actual books. A bright color or something with a bit of texture (they call it "résumé" paper in some copy shops) could work. Experiment with a few papers and see what you like before you print your entire edition.

9   Cut the pages, fold together, and stitch. (Depending on the style and your intention for the

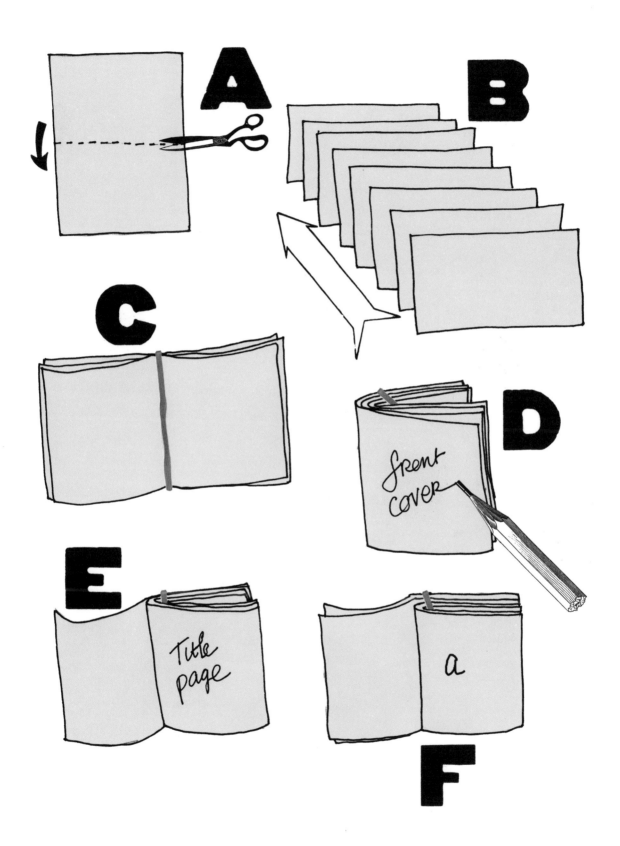

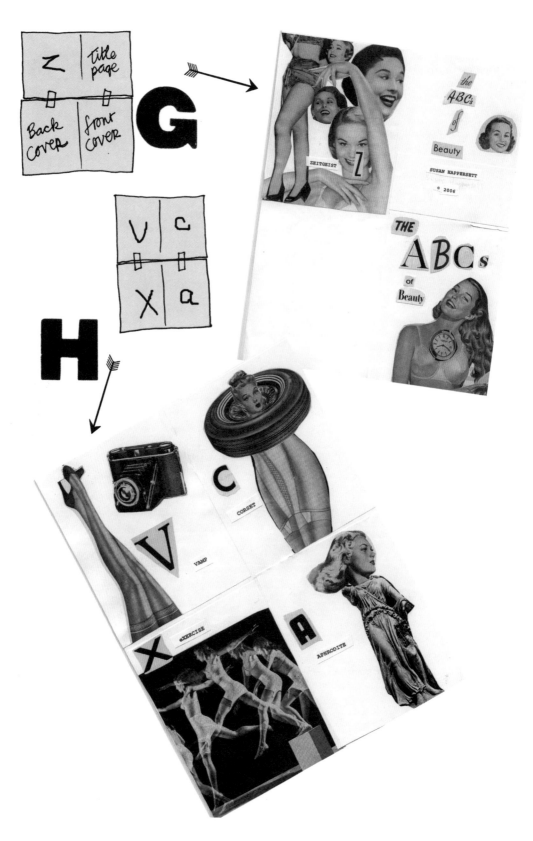

book, you can also staple your pages. To make the staple lie on the fold of the signature, you may need a saddle-stitch machine, which is really just a larger stapler. I am always jamming staplers and find it easier to sew.)

If you are sewing a bunch of books, try sewn staples. Take a long piece of thread (from one shoulder to the opposite extended hand should be long enough) and sew staple-size stitches. You'll have three holes, as with your standard pamphlet stitch, but make them much closer together, $1/2$" (13mm) or so apart in the center of the book. Sewing like this goes quickly because you don't need to keep threading. You can embellish the spine with charms, beads, or little buttons.

STORING PAPER

Do not keep your paper rolled. You can keep it well wrapped under a rug or under a mattress. Keep your eyes open for flat files. Sometimes we have found things like that on the street—in New York, all kinds of wonderful, valuable things are discarded since space is at such a premium. Sometimes flat files are available used or at tag sales when a design studio or print shop is going out of business. As more and more information is stored electronically, more and more file cabinets (and even flat files) are no longer needed and so are available for your burgeoning collection of cool and eclectic bookmaking papers.

10 Once you are sure that your book works, and if you aren't using the outer pages for the cover, you can make a cover from heavier paper and add thin, decorative end sheets. You could also make a collage-pattern end sheet. Sometimes I reduce an image that I like, photocopy it a bunch of times, cut the pages out into different shapes, and make a pattern. This is easy to do on the computer, if you know how.

11 You can make a cover label that is photocopied, cut out, and glued to the cover with a glue stick, double-stick tape, or transfer tape. Burnish the label, protecting it with a clean waste sheet.

Bone-folder debossing around the label can be a nice touch. To bone-folder deboss, you just trace around your image (in this case, the label), rubbing or drawing with a firm stroke of the tip of your bone folder. I have traced and made rubbings of metal rulers, triangles, drafting curves, and coins to create an embossed effect.

The basic page size can, of course, be different. It is good to know the press size and standard paper sizes when you begin to design a book. If you are very rich or don't care how much money you spend, don't bother with this—almost everything can be custom made given enough time and money. But for the rest of us, it makes sense to look at what is available and see what you can do with it. Our letterpress prints a maximum sheet size of 14 x 18" (35.5 x 45.5cm). I sometimes cut paper samples into 14 x 18" (35.5 x 45.5cm) sheets and just fold them various ways to see what pleasing proportions I can find. Somehow working with limitations can get my creative juices flowing. That may be why I am a designer: Rather than being intimidated by a big blank piece of fancy expensive paper, problem solving with this limitation stimulates me.

If you are planning to print your editions with a photocopier, take a piece of the $8 1/2$ x 11" (21.5 x 28cm) paper, check the grain (often this paper will be short grain, to allow it to pass through the rollers of the printer), and fold it a few ways to see what you like best. The largest, widest signature will be $5 1/2$ x $8 1/2$" (14 x 21.5cm), though if you want a square, you can trim to $5 1/2$" (14cm) on both sides. A tall, skinny book would be $4 1/4$ x 11" (10.75 x 30cm), and although it is tricky to fold paper into thirds, you could do it and make a $4 1/4$ x $3 2/3$" (10.75 x 10cm) book.

If you are working with a commercial printer, talk to them about press size and paper size before you plan your book.

The Little Black Cocktail Book

When things got tough making the book you are now reading, Lindsay and I discovered that bourbon helped. My usual drink was single-malt scotch with a glass of water on the side, but the price of scotch went up. I had a bottle of dull scotch, and though some drops of bitters improved it, I was looking for a change.

Once when Lindsay came over, she brought bourbon. We walked by the river and watched the sun set and then bought an orange on the way home. She then did something with that orange and bourbon and bitters, plus a little grated fresh ginger, that was very nice: It was an unsweet version of some classic drink that reminded me of my dad, back in that other era of cocktails.

When I tried making it on my own it was awful, so Lindsay gave me the recipe. We made this book to keep it in.

1   Cut text paper and end sheets a little larger than the envelope. Stack them together and slit the envelope, as shown. {A}

2   Fold a signature of about 4 pages around the envelope.

3   Surround your book with end sheets and the cover, cut a little larger than the interior pages so that the inside doesn't stick out.

YOU WILL NEED

Text-weight paper

Decorative end sheets (marbled paper, for example)

Envelope

Scissors

Black cover paper

Awl

Needle

Thread

Bone folder

Contrasting paper for label

Glue or double-stick tape

Straightedge

4   Punch five holes in the spine with your awl or a sharp, thick needle: one near the top, one near the bottom, one in the middle, and two in between the middle and ends.

5   Start sewing in the middle, front to back, leaving a 4" (10cm) tail. {B}

6   Figure-eight stitch around the in-between and top holes by sewing through the in-between hole first, then through the top hole to the back, and finally back through the in-between hole. Be careful not to split the thread. {C}

7   Skip the middle on your way down, figure-eight stitch the bottom (sew through the in-between hole to the back, sewing to the front through the bottom hole, then sew through the in-between hole again) {D}, sew through the middle hole from the back {E}, and tie a square knot around the long stitch, as shown. {F}

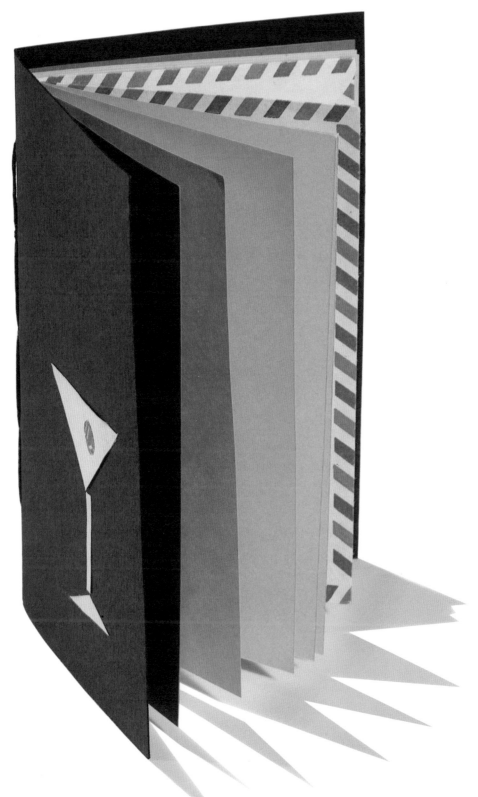

ABOVE: *Lindsay Stadig, The Little Black Cocktail Book.*

8   Make your cover label. I made a martini-glass label for my cocktail book. {G} Here's how to make one for yourself: Using text paper or another thinnish contrasting paper, draw a triangle for the base of the glass, a line for the stem, another triangle for the cup, and a little oval with a tiny circle inside for the olive (you can also cut the olive out of another piece of paper). You can even make a label on top of another label in contrasting colors for a more elegant effect. Paste on the label with a glue stick or double-stick tape, covering your paper with a waste sheet and burnishing well. For a debossed effect, you can trace around it with a bone folder and a straightedge.

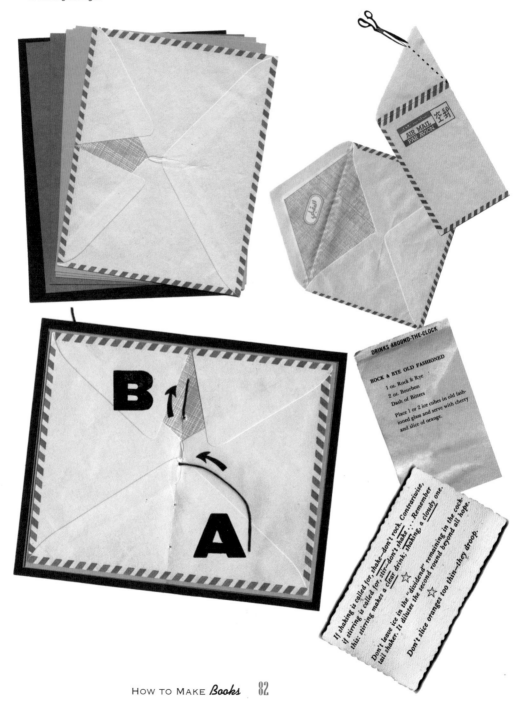

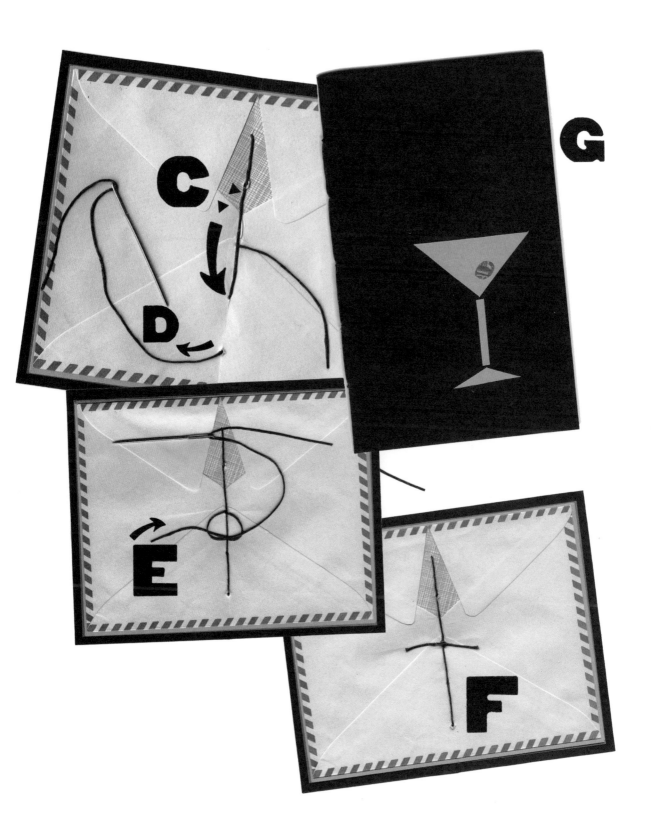

ABOVE: *Cooper Union's Instant Artist Book Class, Combo of Crazy Papers.*

Combo of Crazy Papers

This jazzy little improv book is a tradition when I teach. I get an odd piece of paper from each student, play with them all, fold them together, and stitch them to see what comes out. An installation artist once came to my studio, saw these little books, and said I should hang them all from the ceiling. I see them as portraits of my many classes over the years.

YOU WILL NEED

Assorted paper odds and ends

Needle

Thread

Awl

If you are doing one alone, you could start with a collage-paper set sold from an art store, or just take an odd assortment of papers you have lying around. You can use the three-hole or five-hole stitch, or make up your own version. Some artists I know have worked with take-out menus, junk mail, fliers left on their car windshield wipers—it is fun to take ephemeral materials and make something interesting from them.

If a group is making these together, it would be very interesting to see how a bunch of people could take the same odds and ends and come up with very different results.

This book can be a great exercise to get yourself going. Artist Susan Happersett makes a collage every morning (I'm not sure if it's before or after coffee). That's hard to fit in if you have a family eating breakfast on your kitchen table in the morning before you turn it into a studio in the afternoon. But these little (or huge; it's up to you) improv books could be a variation on that idea—a book a day keeps your muse from going away?

1   Pile your pages and fold them into a one-signature booklet. You can fold and cut your paper to whatever size works and feels right.

2   Turn the pages to see if you like their juxtaposition.

3   Stitch with three, five, or more holes—whatever seems to work with your paper and design.

4   Embellish with beads, buttons, and charms, if they go with your jazzy improv book.

Chapter 5

MUTANT BOOKS

ARTIST BOOKS NEED TO display well in exhibition cases. They also need to function on an intimate level for a single reader. I want my books to be fun to manipulate. Mutant books can work on both levels. They can be sculptures, and at the same time reveal subtle elements to a single viewer in a quiet room.

With this chapter, we begin multisignature bindings. Mutant books require less planning and less precision than other multisignature bindings. The ratio of craft to creativity will change when we begin long stitch and Coptic, which are less intuitive. Before you start these, make books using many pages using the forms that you now know. You've learned the basics—combine them! Sew pamphlets into narrow accordion pleats. Stitch accordions between the pages of a single signature. Add fold-out pages. Make covers of doubled paper that open to reveal accordions. Put books inside books. Build from the inside out.

Experiment with whatever is lying around. Then choose papers that have the strength to stand when you open them: The bigger the book, the heavier the paper. If you go really large, use matt board and make cloth or leather hinges. Use metal or wood and piano hinges if your book is even larger. If you make a camping shelter from a mutant book form, please send a photo!

- -

OVERLEAF: *Purgatory Pie Press and Michael Bartalos,* **Vishnu Crew Stews Vindaloo Anew**. *Die cut, letterpress from linocut and handset type.*
OPPOSITE (ABOVE): *Purgatory Pie Press and Susan Happersett,* **Fibonacci Flower**. *Letterpress from plates and handset type.*
OPPOSITE (BELOW): *Purgatory Pie Press,* **Book Toy Cube**. *Letterpress die cut, handset type and ornaments.*

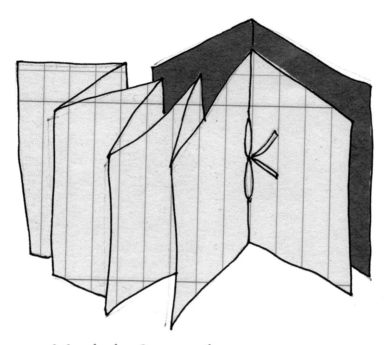

Basic Model Accordion STITCHED INTO COVER

You can attach a cover to an accordion with pamphlet stitch. This stitch also allows you to put decorative end sheets in an accordion. Plus, you can string some beads on the thread as you stitch outside the spine for a sort of book-meets-jewelry touch. Charms on the string ends can be nice. Some artists make tiny versions of these books into pins and pendants.

1   Fold one of the accordion books from chapter 2, and glue hinges, if necessary.

2   Using cover-weight paper, fold a cover with a spine that is thick enough to hold the spine of your accordion. If your paper is long enough, fold flaps into front and back covers to give them more stiffness (and panache).

3   Add a decorative end sheet between the cover and the accordion, if you like.

4   Decide where you will attach your accordion to the cover. It can be stitched at the front or back fold of the spine and through the fold of the first or last page of the accordion. Arrange the accordion so that it fits into your cover, lining up flush with the bottom so the book will stand.

5   Sew with a pamphlet stitch into a fold of the spine, adding beads at the spine or charms on the string ends, if you like.

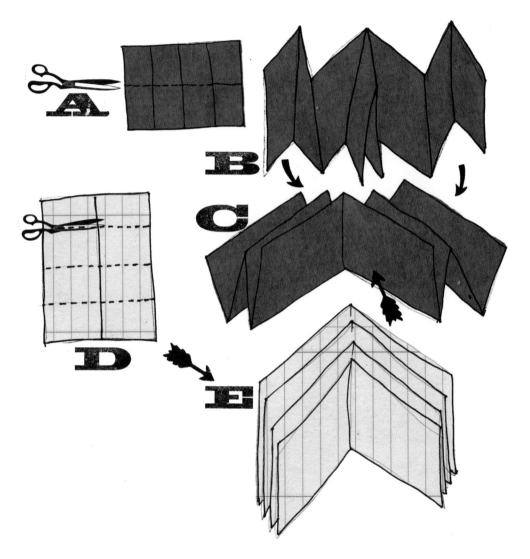

BASIC MODEL ACCORDION COMBO: SECRET BOOK

Here's another variation of the combo theme. Make an instant accordion by folding a piece of 8½ x 11" (21.5 x 28cm) paper in half lengthwise and then in quarters crosswise. {A} Unfold the paper and cut down the long middle fold, leaving the last section attached. Fold this up as an accordion. {B–C} Fold a pamphlet the same way, cutting the pages into four spreads, 8½ x 2¾" (21.5 x 7cm) each. {D} Pile the pamphlet pages on top of each other, inserting them into the center of the accordion between two spreads. {E} Sew with a simple three-hole pamphlet stitch. Accordions and pamphlets can be combined in myriad creative ways—invent your own variations.

Do Si Do

I have always thought of this form as the book version of the square-dance step (which you may have learned in fourth-grade gym class), but I have seen it spelled in some bookbinding guides as *dos à dos*. They are probably from the same root, linguistically as well as theoretically. How group dances and book structures relate to each other could be a whole dissertation. When I went to the Swedish midsummer festival, I was amazed to see dancers twist into tight spiral patterns and then emerge in surprising ways. They reminded me of paper magic toys called flexagons—but that's a subject for my next book.

YOU WILL NEED

Red cover paper, same height and 3 times the width of signature paper

Unsewn signature of heavy, text-weight black paper

Unsewn signature of heavy, text-weight white paper

Bone folder

Linen thread

Needle

Awl

Photo corners, photo-safe tape, or glue

This book shows you one way to make the Do Si Do using two pamphlets, stitched into a Z-fold. I used the Do Si Do when I made the proposal (and promo piece—see first photo) for the very book you are reading: One side was for the illustrations, the other contained the text. For this project, you will make a photo book to house pictures of a pair: two kids or two pets, mom and dad or grandma and grandpa, or before and after, or day and night, or two of just about anything else.

1   Fold the red cover paper into thirds (like a Z). {A, B}

2   Fold two signatures, one with black paper and one with white paper. (This is basically step 1 of the Basic Three-Hole Pamphlet, page 72.) {C}

3   Align the bottom of one signature so that it is flush with the bottom of the cover, matching the fold of the signature with the first fold of the cover, as shown. {D}

4   Using the awl, punch three or five holes through the spine.

5   Sew with pamphlet stitch (shown on page 72). {E}

6   Repeat steps 3 through 5 with the other signature, using the opposite side of the Z-fold cover.

7   Affix pictures of your two people or things onto pages in the different signatures. {F}

If you have three or more children, pets, plants—whatever—that you'd like to make into a book, you can fold a longer cover, W-style, and sew more signatures in. You could, of course, use black or

BELOW: *EK Smith, Do Si Do with Polly and Georgia.*

a neutral paper for the cover and bright or pale color papers for the signatures—or any other combination that you like.

If you want to make an edition of these, you could work them out with a dummy. Refer to steps 1–6 of the Printed Alphabet Book (page 74) for how to make and use a dummy. Then either set them up on a computer to print out, or paste the pictures and photocopy the signatures. They can make excellent holiday cards or party favors.

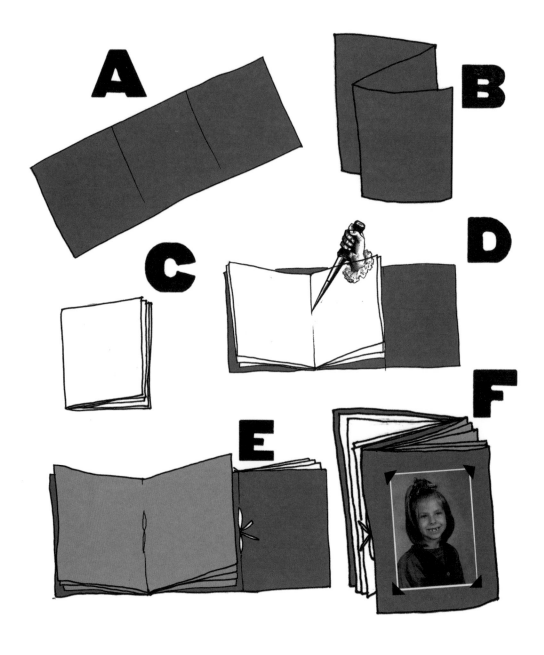

ABOVE: *Lindsay Stadig, sample Travel Journal.*

Travel Journal WITH CONCERTINA AND PAMPHLETS

When I travel, I'm always picking up odds and ends. On a trip to Paris, I fell in love with the small paper bakery bags that wrapped our croissants. Sometimes even the most ordinary paper objects, like ticket stubs, are interesting because they're different. One of my favorite things to do when I travel is to go to pharmacies and grocery stores and just look at the packaging. (On that same trip to Paris, I ended up buying turquoise houndstooth stretch pants in the supermarket. I've almost never worn them, but they were cheap and I was so impressed to find clothes at the *marché*.)

Suellen Glasshouser, an artist who visited my class, told me that she started making books when she lived overseas. She began to make small pieces because she had to work in hotel rooms and little

1 long strip of short-grain cover-weight paper

Text-weight paper

Maps of places you will go (optional)

Vertical envelopes that open at the short end

Bone folder

Needle

Linen thread

Scissors or X-Acto knife

Ribbon or linen tape

apartments instead of in her studio. I was fasci-nated to see that she had made her artist books with some of the same simple bags and pieces of paper that I had loved when I was there.

Even on a road trip in this country, I love the paper ephemera: fliers for private museums, tourist-cave brochures, diner place mats, and anything from Yocco's The Hot Dog King in Allentown, Pennsylvania, which is usually my first stop on a road trip out of New York City. They are the only hot dogs I ever eat—I get the Polish sausages with onions and peppers and Yocco's spicy special sauce. They have sides of piero-gis (in printed paper wrappers), neighborhood dairy chocolate milk, and birch beer. Local color seems like an endangered species, so I love to find some real local things to let me know that I'm somewhere different from the next place. Travel journal scrapbooks are one of the ways to celebrate and preserve these specifics.

1 Fold the strip of cover paper in half along the grain, then decide how big you want your covers to be and fold them back from the edges, leaving a long strip in the middle. {A} *Note:* If you want a heavier cover, you can fold the cover-weight paper in half over the self-cover and glue it. Alternatively, you can make a narrow accordion without covers and attach boards for the covers.

2 Accordion fold the strip between the covers, folding it in half again and again until the entire strip is folded as a 1" (2.5cm) accordion. {B} Reverse folds as necessary so that they fit between the covers. Remember to burnish your folds with your bone folder. {C}

3 Using the text-weight paper, fold signatures for each of the concertina folds. {D} They should be the same height as your concertina covers and a little narrower, so that they don't stick out when the book is closed.

4 You can fold envelopes into the pamphlets. {E}

5 If you have maps of where you are going, you can fold them now into the centerfolds of the signatures. {F} Or add them and other bits of paper from your trip later to make a post-travel scrapbook.

6 Pamphlet-stitch the signatures into the shallow folds of the concertinas.

7 To make a tie to keep your book shut, slit the covers and thread with long ribbons or linen tape.

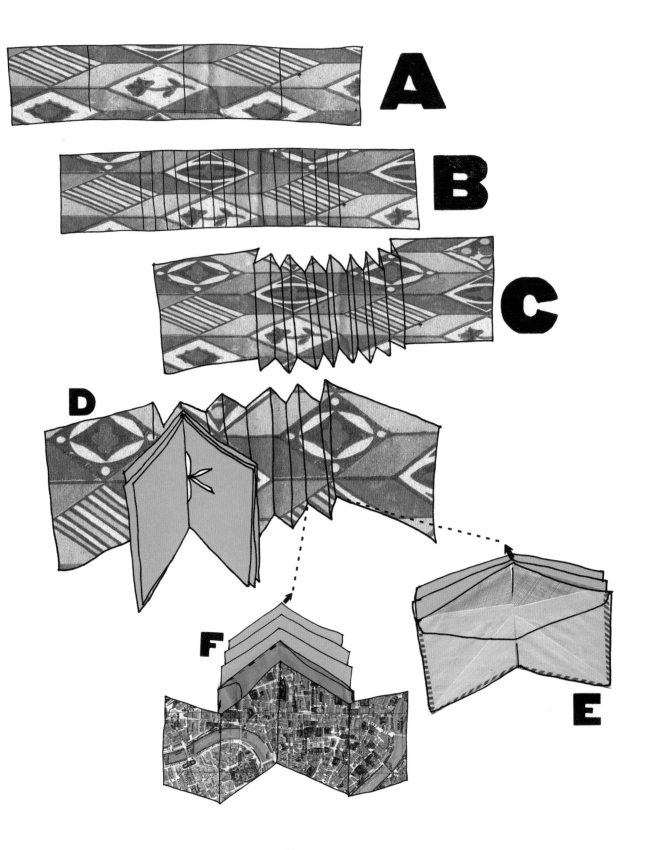

A

B

C

D

E

F

Chapter 6

LONG STITCH

DIKKO AND I FIRST SAW long-stitch books when,

after a few years of making books, we went to Chicago to sell

books to the rare-book librarian at the Newberry Library. While

we were there, we looked up Gary Frost, a book conservator who

did historical research. He introduced us to his protegé, Pam

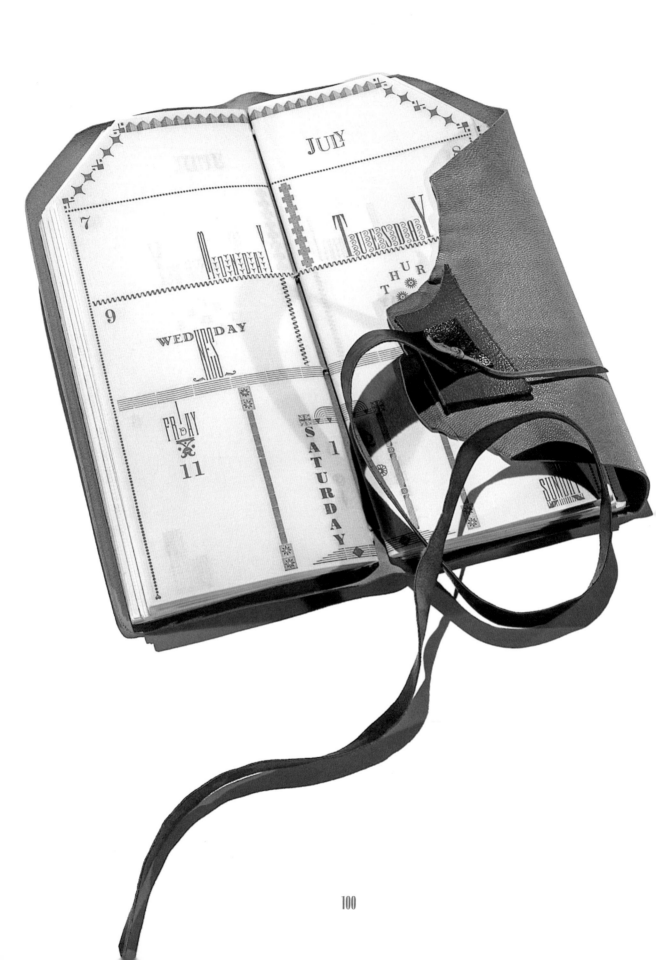

Spitzmueller, who has since gone on to an illustrious career of her own. Pam had a little exhibit at the library. It changed my life. She had taken very old, unusual books and made new versions of their bindings. These old and new books were displayed together. I cannot tell you how important this was for me. Before that, I might have been exposed to these structures, but I was making books with cloth-covered boards and hadn't really noticed other forms.

Hedi Kyle, a well-known inventive binder who taught at the Center for Book Arts in New York City, had bought some unbound datebooks from us. She told me she was planning to bind them in softcover leather. Heidi never got around to binding the datebook, but the idea of softcover leather plus Pam's exhibit of contemporary books made with archaic book structures inspired me. It was the beginning of my thinking about book structures as sculptural forms instead of mere book containers that need decoration to become interesting.

- -

OVERLEAF: *Purgatory Pie Press*, **Leap Year of Fate**. *Unique long-stitch leather with Milagros, letterpress from handset type and linoleum.*
OPPOSITE: *Purgatory Pie Press*, **Dollhouse Datebook**. *Unique long-stitch leather, letterpress from handset metal type and ornaments.*

Cake Box Book

In the early eighties, there was a push for generic grocery packaging. So much money went into the design and printing of packaging, and finally someone hit upon the idea that you could save a lot if everything came in a plain brown wrapper or its equivalent. Thus was born the white box with only a barcode and the bold Helvetica type that said CEREAL or OATMEAL or DOG FOOD. These were interesting at first. Dikko and I even made generic Halloween costumes: We took white paper painters' coveralls, cut out black tape letters that spelled COSTUME, and

LEFT: *EK Smith, sample Cake Box Book.*

taped on barcodes. We marched in the Greenwich Village Halloween parade, and people loved them. Every few seconds a spectator would say, "Look, they're brand X." Eventually we got bored and dropped to the sidelines. On the shelves, generic packaging got boring, too. Within a year, the wonderful colorful boxes were back and proud in the supermarket. Now it's time to celebrate the gorgeousness of box design with make-it-yourself pop art.

YOU WILL NEED

Cake-mix box that is approximately the size and shape of a book (pasta boxes with windows are also fun to use)

Scissors or X-Acto knife and cutting mat

Graph paper with ¼" (6mm) grid

Awl

Paper for folded signatures (graph paper or accountant paper can work well—combine several patterns, if you like). The exact number of pages will depend on the number of signatures and the weight of the paper; see step 8.

Bone folder

Needle (a blunt needle with a large eye works best)

Waxed linen thread

I began seeing box covers sewn into books in 2000. At a time when high craft and the preciousness of artist books was becoming annoying, and book arts seemed like the macramé of the nineties, these frank, simple, funny books were fresh and unpretentious. I have not thrown away a box since, and they are piling up. I like cake-mix boxes especially, with their tempting serving suggestions and glistening frosted cake slices, but you can use any box that is about the size of a hardcover book.

1   Empty the box and gently take it apart at the seams, keeping the book spine—the side to the left of the front—intact.

2   Flatten the box and trim off the top, bottom, and right side pieces, as shown. You can trim the box smaller if that will improve the proportions. {A}

3   Cut a piece of graph paper to the exact size of the spine. Mark the top and number the line intersections across. There will probably be around eight or nine. This number determines how many signatures you will sew. {B}

4   With a pen or pencil, mark a row of sewing holes, one hole for each line intersection, about ½" (13mm) from the top of the spine, as shown. Next mark the bottom holes about ½" (13mm) from the bottom. You will be sewing your signatures to cover these holes. {B}

5   You also need to mark two rows of holes in the middle. Choose where you'd like them to go: If they are asymmetrical, the book will be more foolproof, so this is a good way to do your first book. But also consider the design of the box. There may be places that would look interesting with stitching. Sometimes the nutritional information or ingredients are printed in rectangles that would look nice with stitching. {B}

6   Using the awl, punch these sewing stations into the spine cover, {B} being careful to protect your table with a cutting mat, or board. My kitchen table has a sewing pattern etched in it from one

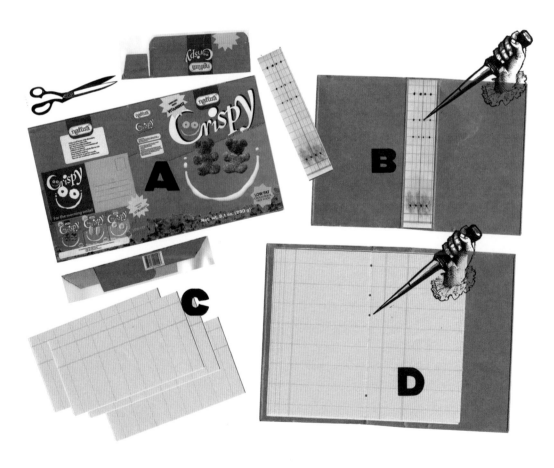

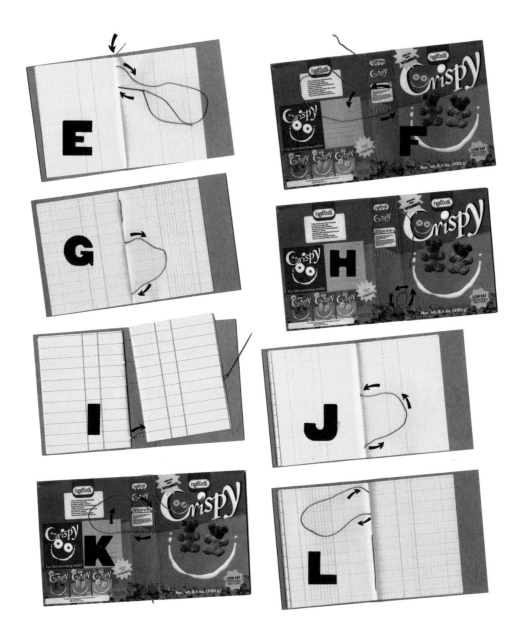

of the first times I did this binding. Some people use old phone books to cut and punch on. Phone books can be great gluing surfaces, too; you just turn the pages as they get gluey.

7   Now count your signatures. For each one, you will need four to eight sheets of paper, depending on its thickness (and your personal taste). {C}

8   Cut your sheets of paper so that the grain runs the length of the book. Each sheet should be the height and almost 2 times the width of the front cover. You need to cut the pages about $1/4$" (6mm) smaller than the cover so they won't hang out after you sew them.

9   Fold your signatures, burnishing the folds with a bone folder as you go.

10 Weight the signatures until they relax.

11 Punch holes into your signatures. Line up one signature with the spine, and mark the holes on the folded edge of the signature with a pencil. Turn it inside out and poke those holes with an awl. Remove one sheet from this signature: This will be your "mother sheet," the hole-punching guide you'll use for the rest of the book. If its holes become too enlarged, replace that sheet with another from this first signature. {D}

12 Insert the mother sheet into your next signature and use it as a guide to punch the holes with your awl. Continue this process with all of your signatures.

Note: If you plan to make several books with the same pattern, you can make a hole punching guide (or gig) by folding a piece of paper the height of the signatures. It doesn't need to be as wide as the signatures. Line up this piece along the graph-paper pattern and transfer the marks

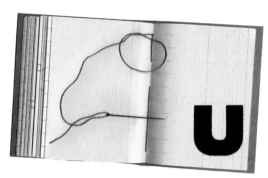

to the spine of the fold on the paper, turn it inside out, and punch the holes with your awl from the inside.

13 When all the holes are punched, put the guide sheets back into the mother signature, which you can still use as one of the book's signatures. Place the guide sheets in the middle of the signature so their larger holes won't show.

14 Line up all your punched signatures, and make sure that the holes on the signatures all match those on the cover.

15 Now prepare to sew. Use a generous length of thread for each signature, with several extra lengths added for good luck. If this thread is exceedingly long, cut it in half. (The thread should not be longer than the distance between one shoulder and your other extended hand.)

16 Start sewing from the outside of the box with the first top hole, and leave a tail of thread, which will eventually be tied, threaded, and hidden inside the book. {E}

Note: Waxed linen thread is very strong. These recycled boxes are not designed for bookbinding, so be aware that you can tear your box with your thread if you tug the wrong way. Keep your tension even, pulling gently in the direction you are sewing. You can also tear through signatures with this thread, so respect its strength.

17 Sew into your first signature, aligning the holes in the spine and signature. Sew out the second hole, back in the third, and then out the last. {E, F, G}

18 Add your second signature at the bottom, sewing into the second signature bottom hole on the spine. {H} Sew in and out until you come out at the top. {I–L}

19 Check the tension. It should be taut but not too tight—you don't want the book to buckle. Tie a square knot with the tail that you left from the beginning. {M}

20 Repeat steps 16 through 19, beginning this time with the third signature top hole to add your third signature. {N–R} At the bottom of the third signature, make a stitch up through the stitch connecting your first and second signature, then sew into the fourth signature hole and add the fourth signature.

21 At the top of the fourth signature, make a stitch like the one at the bottom, sewing down through the stitch connecting your second and third signatures. {S} At the end of every subsequent signature make this stitch; it will eventually form an interesting-looking chain stitch and help control the tension. {T}

22 Continue sewing signatures as before, remembering to add the extra connecting stitch at the top and bottom. {S, T} When you finish the last signature, make a chain stitch and then bring your needle back into that last signature. Secure your thread and bring your needle outside this signature, making a loop and pulling your thread through it, as shown. Repeat this knot (you have just made what's called a "kettle stitch"!) and then stitch out the signature, but stay inside the cover. {U}

23 If you have extra thread, you can make a design with the remainder, stitching into the cover and crisscrossing to make a design that pleases you. When you finish the design, tie off your thread in the most convenient signature with that same loop kettle stitch, bring your thread back out to between the signature and spine, and hide the tail between the signatures.

24 Thread the original tail from the first signature onto a needle and pull it into the inside of the book, hiding it in the spine. {V}

Grocery shopping has never been the same for me. I find myself choosing food for its beautiful box design instead of checking the ingredients—or even what it is. Think of it as choosing a book by its cover. Or more accurately, choosing a cover for your book.

- -

ADDING THREAD

If you run out of thread in the midst of sewing a book, you will need to know how to add thread with a weaver's knot. Tie a loose slipknot into the tail of your almost-gone thread or the end of your new piece of thread. {A, B} Lasso the tail of the other piece of thread through the loop of the slipknot {C} and pull the slipknot hard with a very fast motion—you feel a "pop!" when the threads magically attach together. {D} Pull the two pieces of thread to make sure they stay attached. If they do not, try again. (And if all else fails, attach with a square knot instead.) Trim both tails of the thread.

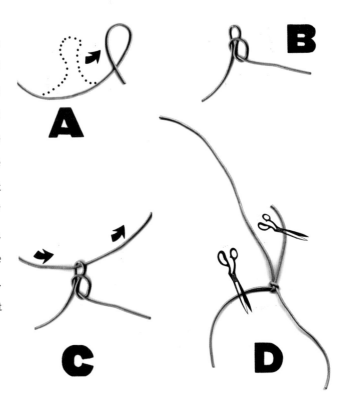

ABOVE: *Purgatory Pie Press,* **007 License to Datebook**. *Long-stitch leather, letterpress with handset type and metal rule.* BELOW: *EK Smith, Leather Journal.*

Leather Journal

For this journal, use leather that is like cover-weight paper—not too floppy but foldable. Recycled leather clothes can work well as long as they are not brittle. Lambskin is not recommended for regular book binding, but I like to use it for long stitch—it has a very nice feel, and the skins are small enough that it's not a big investment in leather. I also like to use cow and calfskins with soft, dull finishes. Look for leather stores that sell scraps by the pound. When I go to one of these places, I take a piece of paper the size of my cover and use that to make sure the scraps are big enough. The odd shapes on the edge of the leather can be trimmed or can become part of the book design—I enjoy the creative feedback from my materials. It slows things down, but the final result is better than anything I could have planned in advance.

1 Fold your signatures, pile them up, and weight them.

2 Wrap scrap paper around the signatures to determine the cover size, then cut your leather to the scrap-paper template.

3 Cut a piece of graph paper to fit the spine, and design your hole pattern as for the Cake Box Book long-stitch bindings (steps 3–6 on page 103). You can either use the same hole placement for all of the signatures or create a design.

4 Punch holes in the spine. Some people line the spine with a piece of heavy paper to support the leather while punching the holes. Remember to always protect your table.

5 Punch holes in signatures, creating a "mother sheet" as for the Cake Box Book (step 11 on page 104).

6 Sew as for the Cake Box Book (steps 14–22 on pages 106–107).

7 When you have finished sewing, try wrapping the extra leather around the book and see what looks good. Trim off any excess, and add ties if you like.

This will be an excellent writing journal to keep in your pocket or bag. I love having a little book with me for the ideas that spring up as I walk through the city.

YOU WILL NEED

Text-weight paper folded into six to ten (or more) signatures

Leather

Sharp scissors or X-Acto knife

Graph paper

Needle

Waxed linen thread

Awl or leather punch

Leather ties or ribbon (optional)

Chapter

7

COPTIC

WHEN I ASKED DIKKO IF HE remembered Reggie,

he said, "You mean that Coptic guy?" I remembered him stop-

ping in at Toni Weil's Tenth Street apartment for hand-ground

coffee the time she showed me how to bind datebooks. Reggie

Walker had discovered an ancient bookbinding from Africa, the

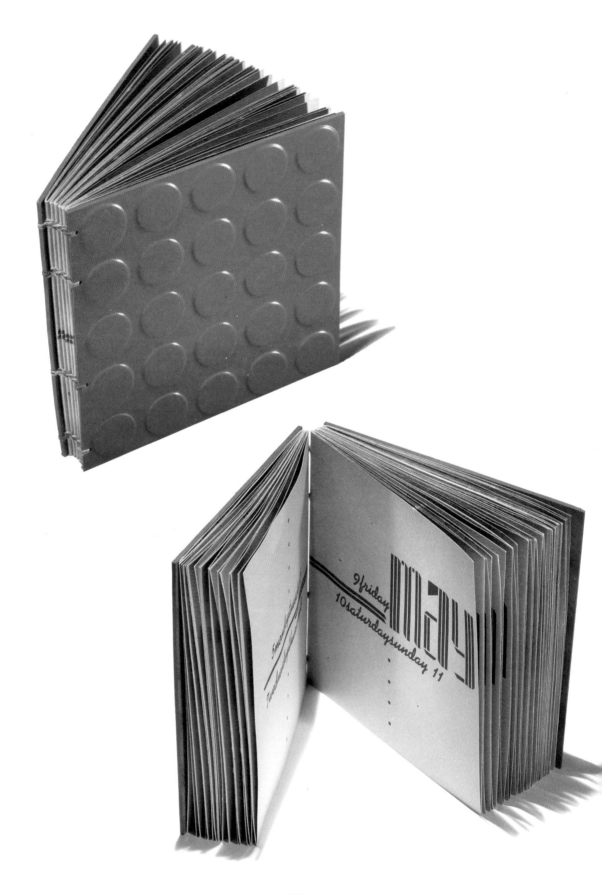

Coptic binding. He didn't want anyone stealing the idea from him. And in his lifetime, they did not.

But fifteen years later, Coptic was the IT binding. I decided to make Coptic-stitch datebooks using covers of painted masonite left over from a project with an abstract painter. The datebooks were running late, as usual. Zahra Partovi was the Coptic expert. I called her in desperation and asked for a lesson. She invited me uptown. My subway got stuck on the way—I was frazzled when I arrived. She sat me on a low chair, eye level with the table. We set the book covers and pierced sections at the edge of the table. She arranged a lamp with a bright bulb so light shone through the pierced holes in the signatures. I started stitching. She said to tug tug tug at every hole to keep the tension even—I ripped my signature. I replaced it with another one and ripped that, too—I was not used to heavy waxed thread. She said, "You must be very relaxed to sew a book." I always think of her when I start to sew an edition. I need to stop worrying, stop thinking about business and teaching and paying bills. I relax into the rhythm of sewing a book.

- -

OVERLEAF: *Purgatory Pie Press, Coptic-bound datebooks with assorted covers.*
OPPOSITE: *Purgatory Pie Press, Coptic-bound datebook. Handset type, letterpress, rubber cover.*

Postcard Coptic Book

Just out of college, I was lonesome for my easy, casual community. I missed my friends who had scattered to the coasts. Long-distance telephone calls were expensive. In those pre–e-mail days, postcards were my way of keeping in touch. I began making my own postcards, writing on the backs of photos that I'd printed, cutting down cereal boxes and large pieces of art, taking the lurid covers off pulp paperbacks. Postcards became my art form. I even started the EK Smith Museum, hoping to be included in an artist postcard mailing list. Although I did not get involved with organized mail-art groups, the EK Smith Museum of found art and an apron collection sent collage postcards as one of its outreach programs.

When I moved to New York, the EK Smith Museum merged with Purgatory Pie Press. The collaborative postcard subscription series was one of my first innovations. In the tradition of letterpress broadsides, but easier to store in a 390-square-foot apartment, postcards were fun. They did not require framing or wall space. So if you, like me, have too many postcards, you can make them into these little books. It is also a low-stakes approach to Coptic binding.

Do not start with your favorite postcard—your first book won't be perfect. I like to use advertising postcards that I pick up free from display racks in trendy restaurants and bars. Of course, some of those are so beautiful that I end up collecting them, too.

YOU WILL NEED

4 postcards

Glue, paste, or archival double-stick tape

Text-weight paper that is twice the width of your postcards (see step 4 for how much you need)

Awl

Curved needle (instructions on page 116)

Waxed linen thread

COVER PREPARATION

1   Choose four postcards: One will be the front, one will be the back, and the other two will line the front and back covers, functioning as end sheets.

2   Using glue or double-stick tape, affix the postcards to their liners to make two covers and end sheets. {A}

3   Punch holes with the awl in the covers about ¹/₄" (6mm) from edge. You will need one hole near the top, one near the bottom, and three in between. If you make them asymmetrical, you will be less likely to sew a signature in backwards or upside down. {B}

ABOVE: *Lindsay Stadig, sample Postcard Coptic Book.*

4 You need six or more signatures for this project, and each signature should consist of two to eight pieces of paper folded, depending on the thickness of the paper.

5 Fold the signatures and weight them until they are relaxed before punching your holes. {C}

PUNCHING

6 Line one signature up with your cover board and lightly mark where the holes should go so that they match the board's holes—this will be your "mother signature," which you will use as a guide. Punch those holes with an awl. {D}

7 Take a page from this signature, setting the signature aside so that you can put the page back later, and use it as a guide for punching the holes in your other signatures. If that page starts to get big holes, replace it with another folded page from the mother signature. When you put these pages back in, put them in the middle so their widened holes won't show. Alternatively, you can make a guide signature from sheets that you don't plan to use in your book. {D}

8 Weight the signatures again so that they relax into their folds before you begin to sew.

SEWING

9 Take a piece of thread the length of all your signatures' spines combined, plus covers, plus a few extra lengths, to be safe. If this is too long to sew with, cut it in half. The thread should not be longer than the distance between one shoulder and the extended hand of the opposite arm.

10 Plan to sew at the edge of a table, using the table for support to keep your pages from ripping. Remember that your thread is very strong and can tear pages and even covers easily. The edge of the table will help with this if you let it. (Here is where I wish I could insert a little video into this book, so you could watch a demo—but with Lindsay's illustrations, it will be almost the same!) {D}

11 Pile your covers and signatures (double-checking that all the holes line up) with the spine facing away from you. Flip the pieces, as you need them, to keep them in order. First, turn your cover and first signature toward you, a little over the edge of the table. If you can, sit low and have light coming toward you to help you see the holes that you punched.

12 Start sewing at the inside of the first signature and through the top hole, leaving a tail of a few inches (5cm). Sew through the first hole in the cover, wrapping the thread around and then sewing back inside your signature. {E} Keeping the needle threaded, tie a square knot, and proceed to the second hole, repeating this step until you get to the last hole. {F–K}

HOW TO CURVE A NEEDLE

1 Grasp a needle with two pliers, one at each end.

2 Hold the needle over a candle flame until it glows red.

3 With a slow, steady pressure, bend the needle. It won't exactly curve but instead will bend in an L shape.

4 Let cool, and then thread it and sew!

13 At the last hole, sew through the board and wrap around, but *do not sew back into the first signature.* Instead, add the second signature, starting at the bottom. {L} Sew in and out the first hole. Now the knitting begins (which is why you need the curved needle). {M}

14 Stitch between the cover and the first signature at that same last hole, picking up the stitches, and then sew back into your hole in the second signature. {N} Sew through the next hole in this signature and repeat this step until you get to the last hole. Make a kettle stitch, as shown, between your cover and first signature, but again, *do not sew back into the last hole of this signature.* {O–Q}

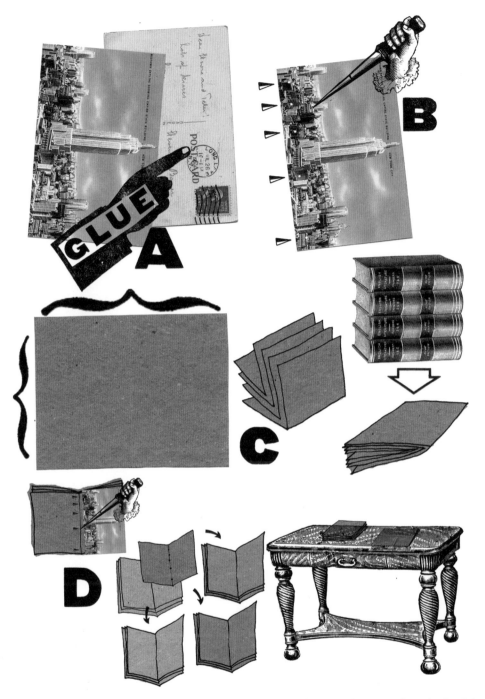

15 Instead, add your next signature and continue knitting the new signatures into the book by bringing the curved needle between the previous two signatures and back into the one you're currently working on. Remember to kettle stitch at the end of each signature before adding a new one. Sew all the signatures but the last one in this way, then proceed to the next step. {R–T}

16 You are going to sew the last signature and the back cover at the same time, which is a little tricky. At first the final signature is just a space holder: You turn it and the cover at the same time, sewing around the cover and through the hole, and then sewing into the hole of the last signature. {U–V}

17 Then sew through the next hole, stitch through the previous signature, wrap around and through the cover, and sew back in the hole. Repeat until you get to the last hole. {W–Y}

18 Sew through the last hole of the last signature, stitch through the previous signature, wrap around and sew through the cover, then sew back in your final hole. Tie off with two kettle stitches, as shown. {Z}

19 Trim your threads and fray the tail with your needle.

You will see that the Coptic stitch made a pattern on the spine. Your first one (like your first scarf if you are a knitter) will have some problems with tension and dropped stitches, unless you are superhuman—in which case, come be my helper in Purgatory! But try another one right away, and you'll get the hang of it. Even if your first attempt came out perfectly, make another one so that your hands remember this stitch. It's really fun to do and nice looking, once you get the feel of it.

Large Sketchbook

One of my favorite college professors was Thad Suits, who taught drawing. He had us keep two sketchbooks. We would turn them in on alternate weeks. He expected us to draw for eight or more hours per week, saying we should spend as much time sketching for his class as we did reading and writing for our history and English classes. I began to draw everywhere, even while watching television. It was one of the best things I ever did. I started designing clothing in those sketchbooks. I used drawings as notes—the process helped me think visually. I began to use a sketchbook as a tool.

I hope you will, too. Alter the size to whatever works best for you. Choose the paper you would like to use—if you want something that won't intimidate you, make one from brown wrapping paper or recycled paper bags. It can be Ingres (named after the French artist known for his drawing) or charcoal paper. You can use different colors in combination, or design some pages to fold out for wide spreads. Or collage on it. Write in it. Take it on trips. Try to recapture that pre–photo-op era, when people paused and took the time to draw.

Coptic binding is versatile. You can use it to make very small and very large books. We use it to make photographers' portfolios. This sketchbook is an example of making a large one—punch your holes every two inches or so. The linked chain stitch on the spine supports your book.

Note: Refer back to the Postcard Coptic Book (page 114) while making your sketchbook for more complete instructions.

YOU WILL NEED

18 x 24" (45.5 x 61cm) long-grain all-purpose paper or drawing paper

Cover material

Awl

Curved needle

Thread

Drill and sanding paper, if using heavy covers

1 Fold your paper in half and cut along the fold to make 18 x 12" (45.5 x 30.5cm) sheets. Fold six or more signatures on the grain with two to four sheets of paper folded into each (depending on paper thickness), to make 9 x 12" (23 x 30.5cm) signatures. Remember to weight your signatures.

2 Decide where you want the holes to be: one about ½" (13mm) from the top, one about ½" (13mm) from the bottom, and five or six in between (they can be 1 to 2" [2.5 to 5 cm] apart).

3   Using an awl, punch holes into one signature to make a "mother signature," which you will use as a guide. Take one sheet from that signature and use it to help you punch the holes in the other signatures. Weight your signatures again before sewing.

4   Cut your covers to the same size as the folded signature pages (9 x 12" [23 x 30.5cm]).

5   Mark the holes on the covers by lining them up with the pierced signatures. The holes should be about ¹/₄" (6mm) from the spine edge of the cover.

6   Punch or drill holes and sand or smooth them as needed so they will not cut your thread.

7   Sew as for the Postcard Coptic book (steps 9–19 on pages 116–118).

When you finish, draw a picture right away. Keeping a daily sketchbook is a great gift for yourself.

Now that you have experience with Coptic binding, you can design your own sketchbook. Use any combination of papers that will inspire your drawings. The great thing about knowing how to make your own books is you will not have to compromise—you can make what you want.

ABOVE: *Kathleen Phelps. Large Sketchbook with linoleum covers.*

COPTIC COVER

Coptic binding has wonderful cover possibilities. I have used Plexiglas, though it was hard to drill, and wood, though it needed sanding and finishing; I thought about glass but was worried that the holes would cut the thread (though if you are or know a slab-glass person who could finish the holes smooth when they are semimolten, that could work). I've used cloth-covered boards, of course, and tried linoleum tiles, and then I started using rubber, which I love. I use rubber whenever I find some that looks good. I've used rubber conveyor-belt material, rubber floor tiles, and escalator stair treads (those were heavy!). One of my students, who lives on Long Island, knew of

an odds-and-ends store that she said carried old rubber floor tiles; sometimes you can get them from building sites. For me, rubber is perfect because I can cut it on the paper guillotine at Purgatory Pie Press, but a shear-style paper cutter works for a small quantity. Rubber also punches easily with a shoemaker's hole punch.

If you don't share my love of rubber, there are still other materials that work nicely with Coptic binding. Kathleen Phelps, a student from my first bookbinding class and the codesigner on this book, cut up paintings on canvas boards. You can recycle old book covers, too. Metal can be fun to experiment with, though remember you must smooth your holes so they don't tear your thread. I'm always thinking about books that will survive a year's banging around in my bag, but if you aren't using your book for an everyday thing like a datebook, it doesn't need to be as sturdy.

The point is, just about anything can work for a cover with Coptic binding. Go nuts. Have fun.

LEFT: *Purgatory Pie Press, datebook with rubber covers.*

Resources

SUPPLIES

Aiko's Art Materials Import, Inc.
www.aikosart.com
Japanese papers. Cool swatch book.

Daniel Smith Art Materials
www.danielsmith.com
Helpful on the phone—good paper catalog.

Hiromi Paper International
www.hiromipaper.com
She can order paper custom-made in Japan.

Kate's Paperie
www.katespaperie.com
The boutique of papers. Some of my former students work here—so you know they're well-informed.

Legion Papers
http://www.legionpaper.com
Distributes art papers. Large-order discounts.

Metalliferous
www.metalliferous.com/catalog.html
Metals, chains, beads, odds and ends.

New York Central Art Supply
www.nycentralart.com
Excellent paper catalog. Knowledgeable staff.

Paper Source
www.paper-source.com
I've found some great papers here.

Pearl Paint
www.pearlpaint.com
Book-art supplies at some locations.

Royalwood Limited
www.royalwoodltd.com
Waxed linen thread. Great service, excellent discounts.

Talas
www.talasonline.com
Serious bookbinding supplier.

ONLINE BOOK ARTS

The Book Arts Web
www.philobiblon.com
Book-arts info and access to archives, links, classes.

The British Library
http://www.bl.uk/onlinegallery/
ttp/ttpbooks.html
"Turn the pages" of amazing historic books.

Canadian Bookbinders and Book Artists Guild
www.cbbag/resourcelistsweb.html
A great resource of resources.

PLACES TO STUDY BOOK ARTS

Book-arts centers are popping up everywhere. Plus, many colleges and community art centers offer book-arts classes. See what you find in your area—you can bring me out as a visiting artist to teach a workshop.

Arrowmont
www.arrowmont.org
I haven't been there, but some of my students have loved it.

Backspace Book Arts
www.backspacebookarts.com
Gallery, classes, and supplies.

Center for Book Arts
www.centerforbookarts.org
This is where it all started, three locations and eight administrators ago.

Chicago Center for the Book and Paper Arts
http://www.colum.edu/centers/bpa/home.html
Classes, exhibits, and advanced degrees.

Cooper Union Continuing Education
www.cooper.edu/ce/bookart.html
My artist-book class is offered three times a year.

Los Angeles Book Arts
www.labookarts.com
Dikko and I lectured and taught here.

Minnesota Center for Book Arts
www.mnbookarts.org
Shop carries Purgatory Pie Press editions, plus excellent supplies. Classes (look for me) and exhibits.

Pacific Center for Book Arts
www.pcba.info
*Exhibits, newsletter, quarterly journal called **Ampersand**.*

Pyramid Atlantic
www.pyramidatlanticartcenter.org
Classes, exhibits, biennial book-arts conference.

The San Francisco Center for the Book
www.sfcb.org
Dikko and I have taught, lectured, and exhibited here.

School of Visual Arts
www.schoolofvisualarts.edu/ce
Learn letterpress printing from the master, Dikko Faust.

Women's Studio Workshop
www.wsworkshop.org
Artist books, classes, grants.

GALLERIES
Printed Matter
www.printedmatter.org
Sells artist books and multiples.

Proteus Gowanus
http://proteusgowanus.com
More than a gallery! Come see our shelf.

Some Books That I Like

Last time I moved, I was desperate with trying to get rid of things. My friend Kathy said, "Throw away your paperback classics, not the weird books you picked up at yard sales and thrift stores—they are irreplaceable. You can always get a new copy of a Faulkner novel."

I didn't throw out the Faulkner (though by now those paperbacks have probably rotted from bad glue and newsprint). But I realized that my best treasures were things I had found. An old Cub Scout manual, a book from the 1930s called *Designing Women*, a 1950s housekeeping manual—they are all wonderful and useful, though you would throw them away if you heeded their advice. And unlike my Faulkner, they are not rotting. Books were bound better back in the day.

Here are some books that I like:

A Book of Surrealist Games
Alastair Brotchie and Mel Gooding
Boston: Shambhala Publications, 1995.
These games can jumpstart ideas and collaborations.

Creating with Paper:
Basic Forms and Variations
Pauline Johnson
Mineola, NY: Dover Publications, 1991.
I grew up with a copy of this book. I love it.

Creative Bookbinding
Pauline Johnson
Mineola, NY: Dover Publications, 1990.
When I learn something new, I usually find it is when I look at this book again.

Japanese Bookbinding:
Instructions from a Master Craftsman
Kojiro Ikegami
Boston: Weatherhill Books, 1986.
The bible of Japanese bookbinding.

Living on the Earth
Alicia Bay Laurel
New York: Random House, 1971.
The ultimate hippie how-to.

Non-Adhesive Binding:
Books Without Paste or Glue
Keith A. Smith
Rochester, NY: Sigma Foundation, 1991.
Not easy reading, but an excellent resource if you know what you're doing. I order copies for my classes.

Thank You

OF COURSE IT TOOK a village, and I want to thank all my students, even the difficult ones, my guest artists, the Purgatory Pie Press interns and volunteers, artists, colleagues, collaborators, curators, collectors, librarians, and funders, my brothers and their families, and my extraordinarily helpful friends: Karen Detrick, Christopher Van Aukin, Tracey Zabar, China Marks, Sarah Ballard, Mindell Dubansky, William Walker, Jessie Nebraska Gifford, Rhea Sanders, Tadashi Mitsui, Sasha Chavchavadze, Maddy Rosenberg, Kathy Troup & Albert Greenberg, Miriam Schaer, Lynda Sherman, Debra Fabrizzi, Megumi Takahashi, Meejin Hong, Sung Mun, Robin Ami Silverberg, Katharine Staelin, Matteo Ames, Stephanie Brody Lederman, Mary Wink, Ed Hutchins, Bill & Vicky Stewart, Diedre Lawrence, Robert Rainwater, Karen Gissony, Virginia Bartow, Janice Ekdahl, Brian Valzania, Bob Ray, Thad Suits, Tom McBride, Natalie Conn, Christine Sarkissian, David Greenstein, Marcia Moore, Susan Happersett, Gertjan VanKempen, Gloria & John Happersett, Gwen Deely, Margaret Richardson, Warren Lehrer, Annette Weintraub, Ann Hjelle, Simon Carr, Mary Austin, Kathleen Burch, Steve Woodall, Jae Rossman, Maria McBride, Charlene McBride, Sue Kazoyan, Margaret Manos, Kyle Forrester, Ricardo Correia, Stan Pinkwas, Chris Neuwirth, Jack Acree & Dina White, Ben Katz , Willard Martin, Emmy Hunter, Peter Evans, Marv Beshore, Joe Osborne, Paul & Patty Faust, Susan King, Becky Bickley, Angela Cappetta, Stephen Guarnaccia, Kathy Caraccio, Jennifer King, Nelson & Blouthy, Eric & Bruce, the rest of the guys at the Tower, Noah Scalin, Jenny Dossin, Jim Tolan, Pat Wilkinson, Chris Neuwirth, Lesley Martin, Dayna Burnett, Louis Ocepek, Chuck Savage, Robert Cohen, Mary Cronquist, Naftali Rottinstreich, Rick Paul, Harvey Redding, Richard Minksy, Griselda Warr, Hedi Kyle, Toni Weil, Susan Share, Ruth & Marvin Sackner, Bob Holman, Lauren Grodstein, Steve Zeitlin, Richard Lilly from The Strand, Lauren Monchik & baby Violet, Christina Schoen, Amy Sly, Lana Le, Rosy Ngo, Shawna Mullen, and everyone I forgot.

To the memories of my parents, Frances & Paul Smith, a painter and a harpsichordist, who gave me a New York City artist's upbringing in central Pennsylvania, as well as to other people I wish were still here: Stephen Corey, who said, "You use all the wrong typefaces and you do it so well"; Tony Zwicker, who said, "You fall between the cracks, and it works for you"; Ted Cronin, Polly Lada-Mocarski, Sharon Gilbert, Suellen Glasshauser, Brian Buzak, Candice Coran, Susie Florence, Peter Anderson, and David March, who bequeathed his pristine collection of Purgatory Pie Press work, including the mailing envelopes, to the Metropolitan Museum of Art.

A City University of New York Faculty Development Grant and ongoing support from the Gifford Foundation helped make this book possible.

For their endless inspiration and forgiveness for the occassional missed bedtime story, Kathleen Phelps would like to thank Éamon and Oona. A special thanks to Roger, for his steadfast support.

Lindsay Stadig thanks her family and friends for their support, enthusiasm, and late-night, last-minute favors. In memory of two inspirational creative forces, John Napolitano and Michael Chase.

About the Author

Esther K. Smith designs limited editions and artist books with Dikko Faust, Purgatory Pie Press's founder, letterpress printer, and hand typographer. Smith and Faust have collaborated with more than seventy other artists and writers.

Purgatory Pie Press has had solo shows at the Victoria and Albert Museum, the Metropolitan Museum of Art, Harvard University, Smith College, and the San Francisco Center for the Book. Purgatory Pie Press books are housed in many rare book collections including the Museum of Modern Art, the Whitney Museum, the National Gallery of Art, the San Francisco Museum of Modern Art, the New York Public Library, Yale University, and the Boston Museum of Fine Arts.

Smith's Artist Books course has been offered at Cooper Union since the early 1990s. She also teaches at City University of New York. As visiting artists, she and Faust teach workshops and lecture internationally. She has curated artist-book exhibitions for the Center for Book Arts (NYC), the Organization of Independent Artists (NYC), and Long Island University (Brooklyn). She and Faust design and print custom jobs and teach privately at Purgatory Pie Press in New York City. PurgatoryPiePress.com

ABOUT THE ILLUSTRATOR, PHOTOGRAPHER, AND DESIGNER

Lindsay Stadig lives in Red Hook, Brooklyn, with piles of victorian ephemera and dusty junk. She studied illustration at Pratt Institute. Currently she splits her time between book arts, decoupage, letterpress projects, bike rides, and window display. LindsayStadig.com

David Michael Zimmerman, a graduate of Rochester Institute of Technology, is an advertising and editorial photographer in New York City. DMZphoto.com

Kathleen Phelps is an art director and designer who lives and works in Brooklyn. Dimension and structure inspire her approach to various forms of design, from architecture and apparel to book binding and graphic design. KathleenPhelpsDesign.com

LEFT TO RIGHT: *Lindsay Stadig, David Michael Zimmerman, Esther Smith, Kathleen Phelps, and Dikko Faust.*

Index